The Rap

The Pretribulational Rapture Viewed from the Bible and the Ancient Church

by
Ken Johnson, Th.D.

The Rapture

Table of Contents

Introduction

In this book we will study the pretribulational Rapture in depth. The pretribulational Rapture is taught by many protestant denominations.

This book is written for Christians who are premillennial in their eschatology. If you are amillennial or postmillennial in your view, please read the book *Ancient Prophesies Revealed* for a complete study on the prophecies of the future Tribulation and Millennial Reign of Jesus Christ.

To study the doctrine of the Rapture we must first define it and then place it in sequence with the other biblical prophecies. Before Jesus returns and establishes His Millennial Kingdom, there will be a period of seven years. This seven-year period is commonly called the Tribulation. A Christian who believes the Rapture will occur at the beginning of the seven-year period is called a pretribulationist. A person who believes the Rapture will occur somewhere in the middle of the seven-year period is called a midtribulationist, and a person who believes the Rapture will take place at the end of the seven-year period is called a posttribulationist.

We will concentrate only on the passages from the Bible, ancient church fathers, ancient rabbis, Dead Sea Scrolls and other ancient manuscripts that refer to a pretribulational rapture of the Church.

Toward the end of the book we will answer the arguments of the midtribulational and posttribulational rapture views. Satan has caused much fear and confusion on this subject. I hope this book will prove to be a small but invaluable guide to debating the Rapture.

An ancient fragment from the early church teaches that toward the end times Christians would fragment into many denominations and become very confused about the Rapture and Second Coming. I believe this word of knowledge has been fulfilled!

> "...when the Messiah's coming is at hand, His disciples will forsake the teaching of the twelve apostles and their faith, their love and their purity, and there will arise much contention about His coming and His appearing..." *AOI fragment*

Structure of this Book

The clearest passage on the pretribulational Rapture of the church is 2 Thessalonians 2; but before we examine that passage, we need to look at other passages that define terms used in 2 Thessalonians 2. This way we can see the teaching clearly.

We will define the Rapture, apostasy, seven-year tribulation period, the Day of the Lord, the Antichrist and his revealing, and the birthpangs. We will then examine what Jesus taught about these things and finally go to 2 Thessalonians 2.

Definitions, common arguments, and Scriptures used by non-pretribulationists are cited in the back of this book. Hopefully, this will be an easy-to-use guide for debating the Rapture of the church.

The Rapture Defined

What is the Rapture of the church? In 1 Thessalonians, the apostle Paul teaches that when our Lord Jesus Christ comes back for His church, all those who died trusting the Messiah will be physically resurrected. When this resurrection occurs, the believers in the Messiah that are still alive will be transformed into glorified creatures. Then the two groups together will meet in the air and go to be with Jesus Christ.

> "For this we say to you by the word of the Lord, that we who are alive and remain until the coming of the Lord, will not precede those who have fallen asleep. For the Lord Himself will descend from heaven with a shout, with the voice of *the* archangel and with the trumpet of God, and the dead in Christ will rise first. Then we who are alive and remain will be caught up together with them in the clouds to meet the Lord in the air, and so we shall always be with the Lord. Therefore comfort one another with these words."
> *1 Thessalonians 4:15-18 NASB*

In this translation the phrase "caught up" is one word in Greek. The Greek word "harpazo" means to be snatched. In Latin the word for snatched is "raptus." This is where we get the modern English word "rapture."

Paul gives us a little more detail in 1 Corinthians. In this passage Paul describes the Rapture as "the changing." He states not all of us *will* "sleep" (or die), but when the resurrection of dead believers occurs, the living believers in Messiah will be changed from our current mortal bodies to glorified, immortal bodies. This all happens in less time than it takes *to* blink.

"Behold, I tell you a mystery; we will not all sleep, but we will all be changed, in a moment, in the twinkling of an eye, at the last trumpet; for the trumpet will sound, and the dead will be raised imperishable, and we will be changed."
1 Corinthians 15:51-52 NASB

In Romans 8 Paul describes the Rapture as the "manifestation of the sons of God," which begins with the "redemption of our bodies."

"But if the Spirit of Him that raised up Jesus from the dead dwell in you, He that raised up Christ from the dead shall also quicken your mortal bodies by His Spirit that dwelleth in you... For the earnest expectation of the creature waiteth for the manifestation of the sons of God... Because the creature itself also shall be delivered from the bondage of corruption into the glorious liberty of the children of God... And not only they, but ourselves also, which have the firstfruits of the Spirit, even we ourselves groan within ourselves, waiting for the adoption, to wit, the redemption of our body."
Romans 8:11,19,21,23

In both 1 Corinthians and Romans, Paul describes this Rapture as changing us from "corruption" to "incorruption." Where did Paul get this teaching about the Rapture/Resurrection? It is taught in the same exact way in Daniel 12.

Daniel on the Rapture
Daniel describes the "time of distress," which is that seven-year period prior to the start of the Messiah's thousand-year reign, saying that it starts with all believers being rescued. The "rescue" is one of the names for the Rapture; see the chart at the end of this section. This will also include

7

believers who have died. The unbelieving dead will resurrect later.

> "Now at that time Michael, the great prince who stands *guard* over the sons of your people, will arise. And there will be a time of distress such as never occurred since there was a nation until that time; and at that time your people, everyone who is found written in the book, will be rescued. Many of those who sleep in the dust of the ground will awake, these to everlasting life, but the others to disgrace *and* everlasting contempt."
> *Daniel 12:1-2 NASB*

The KJV translates "rescued" as "delivered." The Hebrew word means to "escape" or "be rescued."

This "time of distress" is worse that anything that has ever happened before. Modern Christians call this period the tribulation period. This will be defined later.

The prophet Daniel says, "at this time" everyone whose name "is found written in the book" (of life) will be rescued.

The Book of Life is mentioned in Revelation 13:8; 20:15 and other passages. Only believers in the Messiah have their names written in this book. In other words, if your name is in this book, you are a Christian and have eternal life, and will spend eternity with God. If your name is not written in the Lamb's Book of Life, you will spend eternity in hell.

Notice Daniel describes it this way: the believers who are dead (asleep in Jesus) will arise in a glorified state with eternal life, but the rest of the dead will resurrect at a much later time (during the Great White Throne Judgment) to contempt or eternal death.

But it is not just the dead in Christ that are rescued, but *all* the believers. The resurrected dead, along with the "changed" or raptured Christians, are taken from earth to avoid the "time of distress."

John on the Resurrection
The apostle John wrote in the book of Revelation that the first type of resurrection is a resurrection of believers. The second type is of non-believers. This is the exact same thing that the prophet Daniel wrote about.

"And I saw thrones, and they sat upon them, and judgment was given unto them: and I saw the souls of them that were beheaded for the witness of Jesus, and for the word of God, and which had not worshipped the beast, neither his image, neither had received his mark upon their foreheads, or in their hands; and they lived and reigned with Christ a thousand years. But the rest of the dead lived not again until the thousand years were finished. This is the first resurrection. Blessed and holy is he that hath part in the first resurrection: on such the second death hath no power, but they shall be priests of God and of Christ, and shall reign with Him a thousand years."
Revelation 20:4-6

Notice John is not talking about the Rapture, but the resurrection of believers martyred by the Antichrist. We will see in the next chapter that this first type of resurrection happened to many believers when Jesus resurrected.

Those Who Say There is No Rapture
In my experience every time I have come across someone who says they do not believe in "the Rapture" they actually mean they do not believe in a *pretribulational* rapture. Our conversations usually go something like this:

9

The Rapture

Them: I don't believe in a "Rapture," as you guys call it.

Me: What do you think 1 Thessalonians 4 is talking about when it says living Christians will become immortal and then be caught up?

Them: I believe the changing will happen, I just think all that happens at the Second Coming.

Me: All the Christians I know use the term "rapture" to refer to the living saints changing into an immortal form and being caught up. So when I hear someone say they do not believe in the Rapture, I think they are saying that 1 Thessalonians 4 is a lie.

Them: Oh no, I mean I don't believe in the Rapture occurring before the Second Coming.

Me: Well, since you do believe in a "changing" and a "catching away" that happens at the Second Coming, your theological position is called posttribulationism. You believe in a posttribulational rapture.

Them: Maybe so, I just don't like the word "rapture."

Me: Since you believe in the transformation and catching up of living saints recorded in 1 Thessalonians 4; saying you don't believe in the Rapture is like saying you don't believe in Jesus Christ. Then explaining that you actually mean you don't believe that "Christ" is Jesus' last name. You would technically be correct, but saying these things that way will cause Bible-believing Christians to misunderstand you. You will look very foolish and will be allowing Satan to sow confusion through you. Please don't allow that to happen!

10

Names for the Rapture of the Church in Scripture
The Appearing – Hebrews 9:28
The Blessed Hope of "the appearing" – Titus 2:13
The Catching Away – 1 Thessalonians 4:17
The Changing – 1 Corinthians 15:52
The Entering the Bridal Chamber – Isaiah 26:19-21
The Gathering – 2 Thessalonians 2:1
The Manifesting of the Sons of God – Romans 8:18-25
The Mercy – Jude 21
The Receiving – John 14:3
The Redemption of our Bodies – Romans 8:18-25
The Rescue/Deliverance – 1 Thessalonians 1:10
The Rescue/Escape – Daniel 12:1-2
The Revelation of Jesus Christ – 1 Corinthians 1:7; 1 Peter 1:13
The Transformation – Philippians 3:20-21

Past Raptures

The supernatural catching away of a person or group of people has occurred several times in the past. Among these are Enoch, Elijah, Jesus, some first century believers, and the apostle Philip.

Enoch

Enoch witnessed the pre-Flood world. After leading a revival, God decided to take him alive to heaven.

> "And all the days of Enoch were three hundred sixty and five years: And Enoch walked with God: and he was not; for God took him." *Genesis 5:23-24*

> "By faith Enoch was translated that he should not see death; and was not found, because God had translated him: for before his translation he had this testimony, that he pleased God." *Hebrews 11:5*

The *Ancient Seder Olam*, on page 2 refers to Enoch's departure as a rapture.

Elijah

Elijah the prophet lived about the ninth century BC. Second Kings 2:5 implies that all the prophets knew the exact day Elijah would be caught up. This must have been a prophesied event.

> "And it came to pass, as they still went on, and talked, that, behold, there appeared a chariot of fire, and horses of fire, and parted them both asunder; and Elijah went up by a whirlwind into heaven. And Elisha saw it, and he cried, My father, my father, the chariot of Israel, and the horsemen thereof. And he saw him no more:" *2 Kings 2:11-12*

The *Ancient Seder Olam*, on page 97, refers t departure as a rapture.

Jesus

Jesus died and resurrected. After giving instructions to His disciples, Jesus went to the Mount of Olives. From the Mount of Olives Jesus ascended to heaven. An angel told those who watched Him ascend that Jesus would return exactly as they had seen Him go up.

> "And when He had spoken these things, while they beheld, He was taken up; and a cloud received Him out of their sight. And while they looked steadfastly toward heaven as He went up, behold, two men stood by them in white apparel; Which also said, Ye men of Galilee, why stand ye gazing up into heaven? this same Jesus, which is taken up from you into heaven, shall so come in like manner as ye have seen Him go into heaven." *Acts 1:9-11*

First Century Believers

When Jesus died on the cross, many deceased believers resurrected and came out of their graves. Many saw them in Jerusalem; then they ascended. This is probably what the heretics were referring to when they said the Resurrection had already occurred.

> "Jesus, when He had cried again with a loud voice, yielded up the ghost. And, behold, the veil of the temple was rent in twain from the top to the bottom; and the earth did quake, and the rocks rent; And the graves were opened; and many bodies of the saints which slept arose, And came out of the graves after His resurrection, and went into the holy city, and appeared unto many." *Matthew 27:50-53*

Philip

The Holy Spirit led the apostle Philip to witness to an Ethiopian eunuch. Once the Ethiopian understood the gospel and asked to be baptized, Philip baptized him. Then Philip was not changed into an immortal but was instantly raptured to the city of Azotus.

> "And when they were come up out of the water, the Spirit of the Lord caught away Philip, that the eunuch saw him no more: and he went on his way rejoicing. But Philip was found at Azotus: and passing through he preached in all the cities, till he came to Caesarea."
> *Acts 8:39-40*

Conclusion

We have seen Enoch and Elijah raptured without seeing death. We have seen Jesus and some first century believers resurrect and ascend. We have also seen Philip, even though he was not given a glorified body, caught away by the Holy Spirit to the city of Azotus.

With the exception of Philip, all these resurrections were of the first kind, unto eternal life. In contrast with the first resurrection, the second kind of resurrection is called the Second Death. This will occur at the Great White Throne Judgment when the unsaved will be resurrected, judged, and condemned to the lake of fire.

We see this teaching both in Revelation 20:4-6 and Daniel 12:1-4.

Next, we need to look at the prophecy about the seven-year period commonly called the tribulation.

14

The Seven-Year Period

After the children of Israel had forsaken the Lord, the Lord decreed their punishment through Jeremiah the prophet. Nebuchadnezzar would take them captive for seventy years.

"And this whole land shall be a desolation, and an astonishment; and these nations shall serve the king of Babylon seventy years. And it shall come to pass, when seventy years are accomplished, that I will punish the king of Babylon, and that nation, saith the LORD, for their iniquity, and the land of the Chaldeans, and will make it perpetual desolations." *Jeremiah 25:11-12*

The prophet Isaiah predicted that Babylon would be destroyed by a coalition of Medes and Persians. Isaiah even prophesied their leader would be named Cyrus and told exactly how he would conquer the city of Babylon.

"Behold, I will stir up the Medes against them, which shall not regard silver; and as for gold, they shall not delight in it." *Isaiah 13:17*

"That saith of Cyrus, He is My shepherd, and shall perform all My pleasure: even saying to Jerusalem, Thou shalt be built; and to the temple, Thy foundation shall be laid." *Isaiah 44:28*

For complete details on this series of prophecies, see *Ancient Prophecies Revealed.*

The Prophecy of the Seventy Weeks

Daniel 9 tells us that the prophet Daniel realized the prophecies of Jeremiah and Isaiah were about to be fulfilled.

15

The Rapture

Daniel began to pray for God to forgive the Israelites and return them to the land of Israel. While he was praying, the angel Gabriel came to answer his prayer and give Daniel another prophecy.

Gabriel explained that there would be seventy weeks of years between the time of a decree to rebuild the city of Jerusalem and the advent of the Messianic Age. Then the Messiah or "Holy One" would be crowned king of the earth.

> "Seventy weeks are determined upon thy people and upon thy holy city, to finish the transgression, and to make an end of sins, and to make reconciliation for iniquity, and to bring in everlasting righteousness, and to seal up the vision and prophecy, and to anoint the most Holy." *Daniel 9:24*

Then the angel Gabriel predicted that from the decree to rebuild Jerusalem until the Messiah will be seven weeks plus another sixty-two weeks. During the first seven weeks the wall of the city of Jerusalem and the city itself would be rebuilt.

> "Know therefore and understand, that from the going forth of the commandment to restore and to build Jerusalem unto the Messiah the Prince shall be seven weeks, and threescore and two weeks: the street shall be built again, and the wall, even in troublous times. And after threescore and two weeks shall Messiah be cut off, but not for Himself:" *Daniel 9:25-26*

Nehemiah 2:1 recorded that the decree to restore and rebuild Jerusalem occurred in the month of Nissan in the twentieth year of the reign of the Persian king, Artaxerxes. Encyclopedia Britannica gives the date Artaxerxes Longimanus took the Persian throne as July of 465 BC. Therefore, his twentieth year began in July of 445 BC. The

16

month of Nissan following that would have been in March of 444 BC, which was before the twenty-first anniversary of Artaxerxes' reign. The seven weeks, or forty-nine years, ran from Artaxerxes' decree to the year Jerusalem's wall and moat were finished in the period of Ezra and Nehemiah. From that time another sixty-two weeks went by until the Messiah was "cut off," a term meaning "executed."

In the early third century, ancient church father Julius Africanus wrote a book entitled, *"On the Weeks and This Prophecy."* Only fragments remain today; but in fragment 16, he tells us how to calculate the exact date by converting the years to days and changing them from the Jewish prophetical calendar to the Roman calendar used in his day. Julius says that the "seventy weeks" prophecy of Daniel 9 started when Artaxerxes gave the decree in his twentieth year. Years later, Sir Robert Anderson recreated the conversion process for our modern calendar as follows: first, the sixty-nine weeks of years ends with the Messiah's death. If we multiply 69 times 7 this gives us the 483 prophetic years between Artaxerxes' decree and the death of the Messiah.

We convert from the Jewish/prophetic calendar to the Gregorian/Roman calendar this way: we take the 483 years times 360 days per year (the sacred Jewish calendar) and that equals 173,880 days. The 173,880 days on the modern calendar comes out to be 476 years and 21 days (476 x 365.25 = 173,859 and 173,880-173,859 = 21). March 14, 444 BC plus 476 years comes out to be March 14, AD 31. We add one year because there was no "0" year between AD and BC. We then add the 21 days. The final date arrives at April 6, AD 32!

The Rapture

70 Weeks Prophecy

```
        49 years        |          434 years
        7 weeks         |          62 weeks

                        483 years
                        69 weeks

445 BC                                              AD 32
                    173,220 days
```

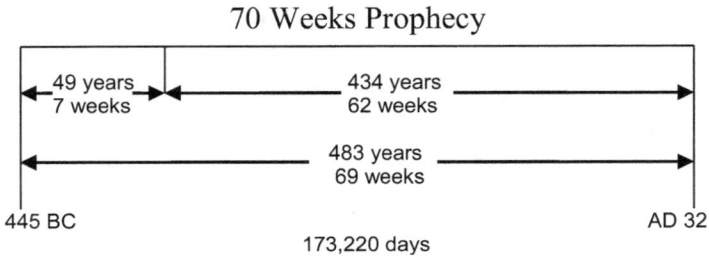

The prophecy states the Messiah will be cut off, not because He deserved it, but to be a sacrifice for our sins. Sometime after the Messiah's death, a prince would come and destroy the sanctuary (or Jewish temple) in Jerusalem, Israel. That destruction would result in a Jewish "war," which would bring the complete "desolation" of the country of Israel. This was also directly prophesied in Daniel 11.

> "And after threescore and two weeks shall Messiah be cut off, but not for Himself: and the people of the prince that shall come shall destroy the city and the sanctuary; and the end thereof shall be with a flood, and unto the end of the war desolations are determined." *Daniel 9:26*

These prophecies were fulfilled in this order: Jesus Christ died on the cross in AD 32. The Roman General, Titus, destroyed the Temple in AD 70. In the year AD 71, the

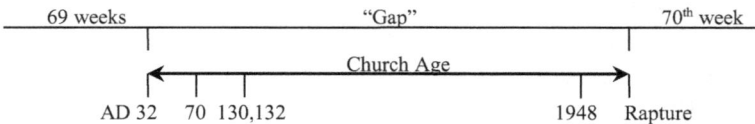

```
   69 weeks                  "Gap"                70th week

                          Church Age

   AD 32   70  130,132                      1948   Rapture
```

18

Seven-Year Period

Roman officer Turnus Rufus fulfilled Micah's prophecy of plowing over the city of Jerusalem. In the year AD 130 the last Jewish revolt occurred that started the great war. It is known historically as the Bar-Kokhba Rebellion. The rebellion was crushed within two years. In AD 132 the Romans officially desolated the country of Israel. The nation of Israel ceased to exist for 1,816 years until the year AD 1948 when the nation was re-established. In 1948 more than ten other prophecies were fulfilled.

Events in the Gap	
Messiah dies	32 AD
Temple destroyed	70 AD
Bar-Kokhba War	130 AD
Israel desolated	132 AD
Israel restored	1948 AD

In Daniel chapter 11, the angel gives a complete list of events dating from 536 BC up to AD 1948. See Appendix C for details on prophecies fulfilled after 1948. Since Daniel predicts the Antichrist will stop the temple sacrifices, there has to be a rebuilt temple. Further, the Jewish people had to return to their homeland.

These are all events in that gap between the 69th and 70th weeks; but what is the gap for? The gap is for gathering Gentiles for His name. The gap is the church age. James quotes the prophecies of Amos and Isaiah revealing this gap is the time of the church age.

"...James answered, saying, Men and brethren, hearken unto me: Simeon hath declared how God at the first did visit the Gentiles, to take out of them a people for His name. And to this agree the words of the prophets; as it is written, After this I will return, and will build again the tabernacle of David, which is fallen down; and I will build again the ruins thereof, and I will set it up: That the residue of men might seek after the Lord, and all the Gentiles, upon whom My name is called, saith the Lord, who doeth all these things." *Acts 15:13-17*

The Rapture
What else could this gap be other than the church age? If it is the church age, and the church age ends with the Rapture, then the Rapture has to be pretribulational.

For those who want to say the gap is the church age *plus* some other period of time, or that the church age continues into the seventieth week, they must admit, then, that the church age is not the gap. For all these prophecies to be pointed to or connected with the seven-year period, that gap must be mentioned in Scripture.

We must ask them, "what is the gap and where is it mentioned in Scripture?" To my knowledge no mid- or post-tribulationist has ever come up with a theory.

The Seventieth Week
In verse 27 we see the Antichrist.

> "And he shall confirm the covenant with many for one week: and in the midst of the week he shall cause the sacrifice and the oblation to cease, and for the overspreading of abominations he shall make it desolate, even until the consummation, and that determined shall be poured upon the desolate." *Daniel 9:27*

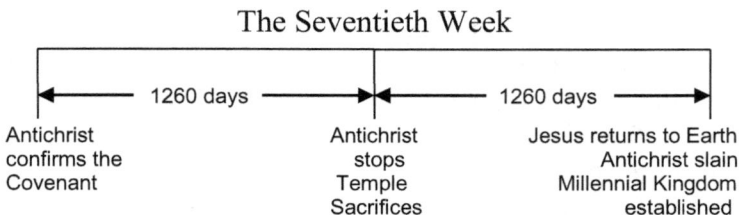

The Seventieth Week

← 1260 days →	← 1260 days →
Antichrist confirms the Covenant	Antichrist stops Temple Sacrifices	Jesus returns to Earth Antichrist slain Millennial Kingdom established

The "he" mentioned here is described exactly the same way by the apostle Paul in 2 Thessalonians 2, where Paul calls
20

him the "man of sin" and the "son of perdition." Modern
Christians call him the Antichrist.

So, Daniel writes the last seven years, the seventieth week,
begins with the Antichrist enforcing a peace covenant. In the
middle of the seven-year period, he will stop the sacrifices
being performed in the newly rebuilt Temple. At *the end* of
the seven-year period the Antichrist will be destroyed by
Jesus when He returns to set up His messianic kingdom.

We can also see this same thought taught in Daniel 7 where
the "son of man," (Jesus) comes and destroys the "beast,"
(the Antichrist) and sets up a kingdom that... "shall not be
destroyed."

Premillennial First Century Church

The first century church fathers were the disciples of the apostles. They had a true faith and doctrine. By the early fourth century the church had begun adopting Gnostic heresy as doctrine.

Here are some of the references from the early church fathers on the end times:

"After the resurrection of the dead, Jesus will personally reign for 1000 years. I was taught this by the apostle John himself." *Papias Fragment 6*

"There will be a future 1000-year-reign of Christ." *Lactantius Epitome of Divine Institutes 72*

"The man of sin, spoken of by Daniel, will rule two (three) times and a half, before the Second Advent... There will be a literal 1000 year reign of Christ... The man of apostasy, who speaks strange things against the Most High, shall venture to do unlawful deeds on the earth against us, the believers." *Justin Martyr Dialogue 32,81,110*

"In 2 Thessalonians, the 'falling away' is an apostasy of faith and there will be a literal rebuilt Temple. In Matthew [24] the 'abomination spoken by Daniel' is the Antichrist sitting in the temple as if he were Christ. The abomination will start in the middle of Daniel's 70th week and last for a literal three years and six months. The little (11th) horn is the Antichrist... The Roman Empire will first be divided and then be dissolved. Ten kings will arise from what used to be the Roman Empire. The Antichrist slays three of the kings and is then the eighth king among them. The kings will destroy Babylon, then give the Babylonian Kingdom to the Beast and put believers to flight. After that the ten nations and the Beast will be destroyed by the coming of the Lord. Daniel's horns are the same as the ten toes. The toes being part of iron and clay mean some will be active and strong, while others weak and inactive and the kings will not agree with each other... The name of the Antichrist equals 666 if spelled out in Greek. Do not even try to find out the name until the ten kings arise. The fourth kingdom seen by Daniel is Rome. The rebuilt temple will be in Jerusalem... These are all literal things, and Christians who allegorize them are immature Christians." *Irenaeus Against Heresies 5.25,26,30,35*

"There will be a 1000-year-reign of Jesus Christ... the millennial reign, Resurrection, and the New Jerusalem are literal. In the Resurrection we shall then be changed in a moment into a substance like the angels... The Antichrist will be a man who sits in a real temple. *Tertullian Marcion 3.5,25; 5:16*

"Paul mentions the Antichrist, as a literal person who works false miracles... There is a literal future Antichrist coming... The prophecies in 1 Thessalonians and Daniel are real prophesies about the end of the world. There will be a literal rebuilt temple." *Origen Against Celsus 2:49; 6:45,46*

Justin Martyr and Irenaeus studied under Polycarp. Polycarp worked with the apostle John for over twenty years in ministry. Irenaeus also testifies that he occasionally saw the apostle John himself.

We can see premillennialism was the standard teaching by the church fathers from Papias in AD 70 to Lactantius in about AD 285.

The Rapture

It wasn't until the fourth century that the church, as a whole, changed its doctrine from premillennialism to amillennialism. This event even has a name. It is called the Schism of Nepos. See *Ancient Prophecies Revealed* for full details on this and many other prophecies.

Now let's look at the Day of the Lord and other terms relating to it.

Day of the Lord

To see when the Rapture occurs, we need to define the terms used by Jesus, Paul, and the others. What exactly is the Day of the Lord, the Day of Christ, the Day of Wrath, the Day of Indignation, the Great and Terrible Day of the Lord, and the Day of the Wrath of the Lamb? Are they all the same thing; or do they represent different time periods?

Day of the Lord
Some have thought "the Day of the Lord" refers to the seven-year tribulation; others, the last half of the seven years. Still others thought it referred to the battle of Armageddon at Christ's return. If we look at all the Minor Prophets, we can see each is describing a *point* inside of that seven–year period.

Joel 3:12-14, for instance, starts talking about the Day of the Lord and then just describes the Battle of Armageddon. Other minor prophets describe the fire and plagues. Joel 1:6 and 2:2-10 describe the invading army in the middle of the seven-year period. Amos 5, however, mentions that the animals will attack during the Day of the Lord.

> "Woe unto you that desire the day of the LORD! to what end is it for you? the day of the LORD is darkness, and not light. As if a man did flee from a lion, and a bear met him; or went into the house, and leaned his hand on the wall, and a serpent bit him."
> *Amos 5:18-19*

If we compare these prophecies with Revelation 6, we see that the animals attack during the Fourth Seal, which is in the *first half* of the seven-year period.

> "And when he had opened the fourth seal, I heard the voice of the fourth beast say, Come and see. And I

The Rapture
> looked, and behold a pale horse: and his name that sat
> on him was Death, and Hell followed with him. And
> power was given unto them over the fourth part of the
> earth, to kill with sword, and with hunger, and with
> death, and with the beasts of the earth."
> *Revelation 6:7-8*

This should prove concussively that the Day of the Lord is the whole seven-year period.

Day of Christ
Paul uses the phrase "Day of Christ" in 2 Thessalonians 2 to refer to the time that the son of perdition, or Antichrist, will rise to power, sit in the Temple, and be destroyed at Christ's return.

> "...the day of Christ ... shall not come, except there
> come a falling away first, and that man of sin be
> revealed, the son of perdition; Who opposeth and
> exalteth himself above all that is called God, or that is
> worshipped; so that he as God sitteth in the temple of
> God, shewing himself that he is God... whom the
> Lord shall consume with the spirit of his mouth, and
> shall destroy with the brightness of his coming:"
> *2 Thessalonians 2:2-4,8*

So, the Day of the Lord and the Day of Christ are two terms that both refer to the seven-year period.

Day of Wrath
God can pour out wrath on anyone He chooses and at any time. He has done so in the past numerous times, but what is the Day of Wrath?

Romans 2:5-9 describes the time when God's wrath is poured out on the wicked, but the righteous get eternal life. So, this includes the time of the Rapture and Day of the

26

Day of the Lord
Lord. Zephaniah 1:14-15 seems to show the Day of Wrath to
be another name for the Day of the Lord.

The Seventieth Week

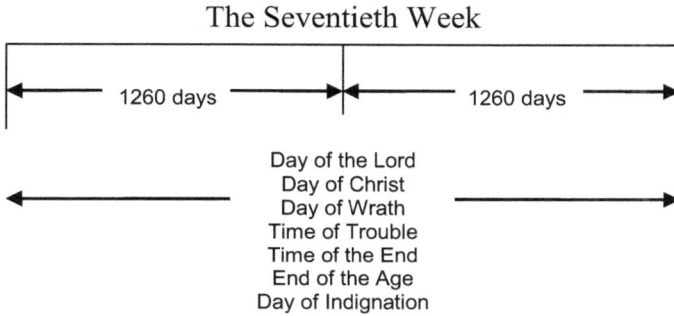

Time of Trouble
Daniel 12 describes a time of trouble. The time of trouble
begins with the rescue and resurrection of believers. It occurs
"at that time," which refers to the end time mentioned in the
previous chapter. In chapter 11 we see the rise and fall of the
Antichrist, including his war with Egypt. This proves the
Time of Trouble consists of the whole seven-year period.

End of the Age / Time of the End
In Matthew 24 Jesus talked about the "time of the end"
taking place after the birth pangs, when the abomination
occurs. Jesus explained this in response to the disciples
asking when the end of the age would occur. The term "end
of the age" is a reference to Daniel 11. Daniel described the
rise and fall of the Antichrist, including the war he will fight
with Egypt. The Egyptian war will occur during the first
three and a half years of the seven-year period. This shows
the terms the "time of the end" and the "end of the age" both
refer to the whole seven-year period.

27

The Rapture
Daniel 12 records that Michael will stand up and the Rapture/Resurrection will occur at the beginning of the time of the end. Daniel 12:7 explains there will be three and a half years between the beginning, Rapture/Resurrection, and the time when the Antichrist scatters the holy people. Next the purification (also called the purging, and Great Tribulation) occurs in verse 10. Then Daniel states that from the time the abomination is set up (which starts the Great Tribulation) to the time the Antichrist is destroyed will be another 1290 days. So, Daniel 12 also clearly shows the "time of the end" is the seven-year period.

The Day of Indignation
The term "the Day of Indignation" appears in Ezekiel 22:24 as the day when the nations will be melted by the fire of His wrath. According to Zephaniah, "the indignation" appears to be the Battle of Armageddon at the end of the seven years. This could be just the wrath of the Lamb or the whole seven-year period.

> "The great day of the LORD is near, it is near, and hasteth greatly, even the voice of the day of the LORD: the mighty man shall cry there bitterly. That day is a day of wrath, a day of trouble and distress, a day of wasteness and desolation, a day of darkness and gloominess, a day of clouds and thick darkness,"
> Zephaniah 1:14-15

The prophet Isaiah wrote that he knew he would resurrect with the other believers and they would all go into the "chedar" (wedding chambers) until the "indignation" was over. Both the "wrath" and "indignation" appear to be terms for the "Day of the Lord."

> "Thy dead men shall live, together with my dead body shall they arise. Awake and sing, ye that dwell in dust: for thy dew is as the dew of herbs, and the

earth shall cast out the dead. Come, my people, enter thou into thy chambers, and shut thy doors about thee: hide thyself as it were for a little moment, until the indignation be overpast." *Isaiah 26:19-20*

Days of Vengeance

Luke 23:21-24 shows "the wrath" includes being led away captive, killed by the sword, and God's wrath being poured out. These events appear to begin after the armies gather around Jerusalem and the Jews are told to flee. So, this would occur during the last half of the seven-year period.

The Seventieth Week

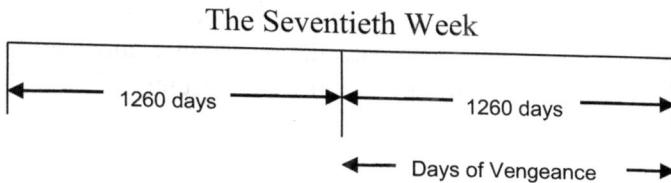

1260 days   1260 days

◄─── Days of Vengeance ───►

Great Tribulation

In Matthew 24:24 and Mark 13:19 the Great Tribulation seems to refer to the great persecution of the Antichrist. This will occur right after the abomination of desolation is set up and right before the sun goes dark and the Lamb's wrath falls. So, this is the beginning of the last half of the seven-year period.

The Seventieth Week

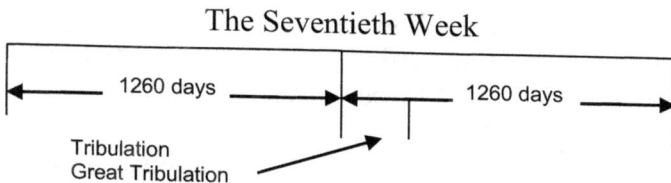

1260 days   1260 days

Tribulation
Great Tribulation

The Rapture
Tribulation
The word "tribulation" means persecution in many places in the Bible. Here are just a few Biblical passages that speak of Christians going through tribulation. Again, substituting the modern word "persecution" for the more archaic English word "tribulation," will make these passages much clearer.

"These things I have spoken you, that in Me you may have peace. In the world you will have tribulation; but be of good cheer, I have overcome the world." *John 16:33 NKJV*

"And not only *that*, but we also glory in tribulations, knowing that tribulation produces perseverance; and perseverance, character; and character, hope." *Romans 5:3 NKJV*

"Blessed be the God and Father of our Lord Jesus Christ, the Father of mercies and God of all comfort, who comforts us in all our tribulation, that we may be able to comfort those who are in any trouble, with the comfort with which we ourselves are comforted by God." *2 Corinthians 1:3-4 NKJV*

"For I consider that the sufferings of this present time are not worthy to be compared with the glory which shall be revealed in us." *Romans 8:18 NKJV*

"And you became followers of us and of the Lord, having received the word in much affliction, with joy of the Holy Spirit." *1 Thessalonians 1:6 NKJV*

It is often asked: if other Christians endure persecution, why do pretribulationists think they will escape without any persecution? The problem with that statement is that all Christians agree the Scriptures state we will suffer persecution. But what the mid- and posttribulationists fail to realize, is that there will be a great persecution that occurs inside the seven-year period.

A more accurate question might be: Why do mid- and posttribulationists think Christians have to go through every single instance of persecution that has ever occurred or will occur on this planet? Just because there is one more persecution or tribulation to occur, doesn't prove who is persecuted or how long it will last. The Nazi persecution was primarily directed against the Jews, not Christians.

Even though the word "rapture" is found only in the Latin Bible, we still use the Latin term to label the "catching up." In the same way, the word "tribulation" was adopted to describe the seven-year period which contains the most severe persecution (tribulation) of all time.

The Lamb's Wrath
This is the time when Jesus, who is the Lamb, pours out His wrath possibly in reaction to the severe persecution of the Antichrist. The Lamb's Wrath is defined in Revelation 6:16-17 and 15:1. It takes place during the time of the trumpet and bowl judgments.

The Seventieth Week

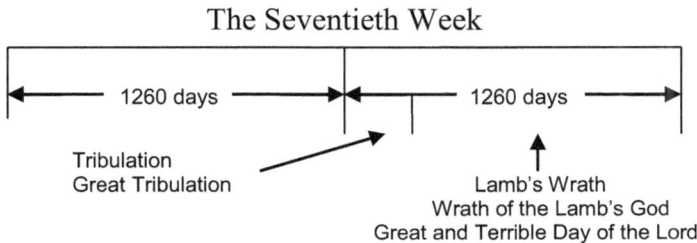

Tribulation
Great Tribulation

Lamb's Wrath
Wrath of the Lamb's God
Great and Terrible Day of the Lord

1260 days   1260 days

The Rapture
Great and Terrible Day of the Lord
This phrase is found only twice in the Old Testament. In both cases it is speaking of a time within the second half of the seven-year period.

"Behold, I will send you Elijah the prophet before the coming of the great and dreadful day of the LORD:" *Malachi 4:5*

"The sun shall be turned into darkness, and the moon into blood, before the great and terrible day of the LORD come." *Joel 2:31*

The sun going dark marks the middle of the seven-year period. So "the great and terrible day" occurs during the second half of the seven-year period. Elijah prophesies for 1260 days and is killed. His death occurs at the end of the sixth trump in Revelation 11:1-14. This means his ministry begins in the first half of the seven-year period. This also proves "the great and terrible day" is different from the general Day of the Lord.

Thief in the Night
In 1 Thessalonians 5, Paul says the Day of the Lord comes as a thief in the night. We have seen that the term the Day of the Lord describes the entire seven-year period. We have also seen that if you witness the revealing of the Antichrist, you will know that exactly 1260 days later will be the middle of the seven-year period. You would also know that 1260 days after that Jesus will return to earth and destroy the Antichrist. This will result in the end of the Day of the Lord and the establishment of the Messianic kingdom.

The only thing we can't know is the *start* of the seven-year period, the day the Antichrist is revealed. So it will come unexpectedly - like a thief in the night.

Unexpected Destruction or Unexpected Rapture?
First Thessalonians 5 says the "Day of the Lord" will come as a "thief in the night" to non-Christians. This means unexpected disaster is poured out on them. That day will not overtake Christians like a thief. This means we will not be hit unexpectedly with sudden destruction *because we shall escape.*

"For yourselves know perfectly that the day of the Lord so cometh as a thief in the night. For when they shall say, Peace and safety; then sudden destruction cometh upon them, as travail upon a woman with child; and they shall not escape. But ye, brethren, are not in darkness, that that day should overtake you as a thief." *1 Thessalonians 5:2-4*

Luke 21 says Christians will not be caught unawares by "that Day," which is a snare to "all" who dwell over the "whole" earth. We will escape by standing before the Son of Man in heaven when we are raptured.

"And take heed to yourselves, lest at any time your hearts be overcharged with surfeiting, and drunkenness, and cares of this life, and so that day come upon you unawares. For as a snare shall it come on all them that dwell on the face of the whole earth. Watch ye therefore, and pray always, that ye may be accounted worthy to escape all these things that shall come to pass, and to stand before the Son of man." *Luke 21:34-36*

No one can escape if they are still on earth. The only means of escape is to leave earth.

Conclusion
We have seven separate terms that clearly refer to the seven-year period: the Day of the Lord, the Day of Christ, the Day

The Rapture
of Wrath, the Time of Trouble, the Time of the End, the End
of the Age, and the Day of Indignation.

The Seventieth Week

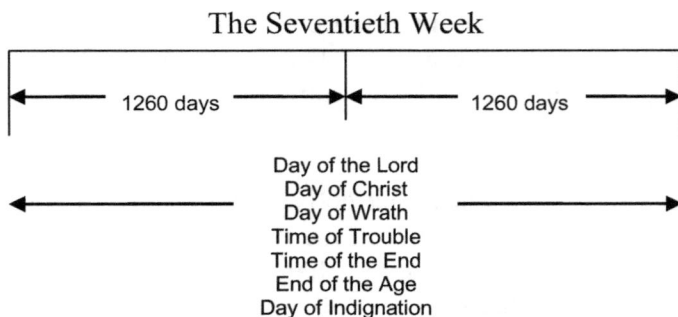

←——— 1260 days ———→	←——— 1260 days ———→

Day of the Lord
Day of Christ
Day of Wrath
Time of Trouble
Time of the End
End of the Age
Day of Indignation

This offers conclusive proof that the Day of the Lord is the entire seven-year period. Now we will proceed to prove the Antichrist is revealed at the beginning of the seven-year period or the Day of the Lord.

Revealing of the Antichrist

When does the Antichrist come on the scene of human history? The Apostle Paul describes the time when he will be finally revealed to everyone on earth.

In 2 Thessalonians 2:1-8 Paul writes about the Antichrist's revelation, the fact that he declares himself to be God incarnate, and his ultimate destruction by Jesus when our Lord returns to earth to set up His millennial reign.

Many Christians will compare this passage with Daniel 9:27 in mind. The Antichrist will be revealed when he confirms the peace covenant at the beginning of the seven-year period. Then in the middle of the seven years he will stop the temple sacrifices and at the end of the seven years the Antichrist will be destroyed.

The Seventieth Week

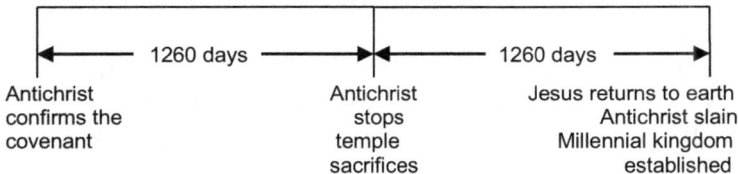

◄——— 1260 days ———►	◄——— 1260 days ———►
Antichrist confirms the covenant	Antichrist stops temple sacrifices	Jesus returns to earth Antichrist slain Millennial kingdom established

Some have wondered if this passage means the Antichrist will be revealed when he sits in the temple in the middle of the seven years.

If the Rapture occurs at the revelation of the Antichrist, it is important that we first determine when the Antichrist will be revealed. If it is at the beginning of the seven-years, then there is a pretribulational rapture; but if it occurs at the

The Rapture
middle, then we may have a midtribulational rapture, sometimes called a pre-wrath rapture.

So, is it at the beginning or middle of the seven-year period?

Some have argued that so far all the peace covenants brokered between Israel and its surrounding nations have been designed for seven years. If that were the only thing to look for, that would make it impossible to identify the true Antichrist at the beginning of the seven years. But, thankfully, that is only one of the many prophecies.

Prophecy 1 – Jewish People Return Home
Since the Antichrist sits in a rebuilt Jewish temple, this also predicts the Jews must return to the ancient land of Israel. This was prophesied in many Old Testament passages and was fulfilled in AD 1948.

> "And it shall come to pass in that day, that the Lord shall set His hand again the second time to recover the remnant of His people, which shall be left, from Assyria, and from Egypt, and from Pathros, and from Cush, and from Elam, and from Shinar, and from Hamath, and from the islands of the sea. And He shall set up an ensign for the nations, and shall assemble the outcasts of Israel, and gather together the dispersed of Judah from the four corners of the earth." *Isaiah 11:11-12*

Prophecy 2 – Temple Ordered Rebuilt
Daniel 9:27 and 2 Thessalonians 2:4 predict the Antichrist will desecrate the Jewish temple. Therefore, a new Jewish temple must be built in Jerusalem, Israel.

> "Who opposeth and exalteth himself above all that is called God, or that is worshipped; so that he as God

Revealing of the Antichrist
sitteth in the temple of God, shewing himself that he is God." *2 Thessalonians 2:4*

Prophecy 3 – Ten Nations Arise

There will be a coalition of ten nations ruling the Middle East at that time. for a detailed discussion on who the nations are and how they come into power, see *Ancient Prophecies Revealed.*

"And the ten horns out of this kingdom are ten kings that shall arise: and another shall rise after them; and he shall be diverse from the first, and he shall subdue three kings." *Daniel 7:24*

Prophecy 4 – Antichrist: Leader of the Ten Nations

Antichrist will become the head of the ten nations through peace and deception, not war.

"And through his policy also he shall cause craft to prosper in his hand; and he shall magnify himself in his heart, and by peace shall destroy many: he shall also stand up against the Prince of princes; but he shall be broken without hand." *Daniel 8:25*

Prophecy 5 – Antichrist's name equals 666

We are told the Antichrist's name will equal 666 when spelled out in Greek.

"And he causeth all, both small and great, rich and poor, free and bond, to receive a mark in their right hand, or in their foreheads: And that no man might buy or sell, save he that had the mark, or the name of the beast, or the number of his name. Here is wisdom. Let him that hath understanding count the number of the beast: for it is the number of a man; and his number is six hundred threescore and six."
Revelation 13:16-18

The Rapture
"Those men who saw John face to face bearing their testimony [to it]; while reason also leads us to conclude that the number of the name of the beast, [if reckoned] according to the Greek mode of calculation by the [value of] the letters contained in it, will amount to six hundred and sixty and six... But, knowing the sure number declared by Scripture, that is, six hundred sixty and six, let them await, in the first place, the division of the kingdom into ten; then, in the next place, when these kings are reigning, and beginning to set their affairs in order, and advance their kingdom, [let them learn] to acknowledge that he who shall come claiming the kingdom for himself, and shall terrify those men of whom we have been speaking, having a name containing the aforesaid number, is truly the abomination of desolation."
Irenaeus' Against Heresies 5.30

Prophecy 6 – Antichrist, King of the North Country
He will be the leader of a country north of Israel.

"And at the time of the end shall the king of the south push at him: and the king of the north shall come against him like a whirlwind, with chariots, and with horsemen, and with many ships; and he shall enter into the countries, and shall overflow and pass over."
Daniel 11:40

Prophecy 7 – Antichrist Will Enforce the Covenant
He will enforce the peace covenant by sending in troops. The word "confirm" does not mean to sign or broker a new deal; it means to enforce a covenant already established but never acted on.

"And he shall confirm the covenant with many for one week: and in the midst of the week he shall cause the sacrifice and the oblation to cease, and for the

overspreading of abominations he shall make it desolate, even until the consummation, and that determined shall be poured upon the desolate."
Daniel 9:27

Prophecy 8 – Egypt will Attack the Antichrist's Armies

When the Antichrist sends in troops to enforce the peace covenant, this action will aggravate the nation of Egypt causing Egypt to attack the Antichrist's armies.

"And at the time of the end shall the king of the south push at him: and the king of the north shall come against him like a whirlwind, with chariots, and with horsemen, and with many ships; and he shall enter into the countries, and shall overflow and pass over."
Daniel 11:40

Prophecy 9 – Egypt Destroyed

The Antichrist will respond by completely crushing the Egyptian armies. The Antichrist will then take over Egypt and two other countries of the ten nations that sided with Egypt.

"He shall stretch forth his hand also upon the countries: and the land of Egypt shall not escape."
Daniel 11:42

Prophecy 10 – Nile River Dries Up

The Antichrist will destroy Egypt and the Nile River will run dry because of it.

"And he shall pass through the sea with affliction, and shall smite the waves in the sea, and all the deeps of the river shall dry up: and the pride of Assyria shall be brought down, and the sceptre of Egypt shall depart away." *Zechariah 10:11*

The Rapture

> "And the Egyptians will I give over into the hand of a cruel lord; and a fierce king shall rule over them, saith the Lord, the LORD of hosts. And the waters shall fail from the sea, and the river shall be wasted and dried up." *Isaiah 19:4-5*

If real Christians were still here at that time, we could quickly identify the Antichrist.

Putting the Ten Prophecies Together
Just these ten prophecies alone would clearly identify the Antichrist. We must remember there are over *eighty* prophecies about the Antichrist and the seven-year tribulation. See *Ancient Prophecies Revealed* for full details.

Presidents Jimmy Carter, Ronald Reagan, and George Bush each brokered a seven-year peace covenant between Israel and other Muslim nations, including Egypt. None of them could have been the Antichrist. Did any of their names equal 666 in Greek or Hebrew? Once the peace covenant was signed, did any of them send in troops to enforce it? Did Egypt instantly attack the coalition troops and did our troops invade and completely destroy the nation of Egypt? Is the Nile River still there? Has the temple been rebuilt? Were Jimmy Carter, Ronald Reagan, or George Bush a king or president of a country to the north of the nation of Israel?

If US president Donald Trump facilitates a seven-year peace agreement between the Israelis and Palestinians, he still does not qualify as the Antichrist. Is President Trump the king or president of a nation to the north of the country of Israel? His name does not equal 666 when spelled out in Greek or Hebrew.

Some of the midtribulationists ask: what if you are wrong and the Rapture does not happen at the beginning of the seven-year tribulation? Aren't you afraid you might cause
40

someone to lose their faith when they see your teaching did not come to pass?

Not at all! If they see nine of the ten prophecies happen, I think it would strengthen their faith and make them wonder why they had one out of order. It would then drive them back to Scripture to search for the time of the Rapture.

Conclusion
Since there are so many prophecies that occur at the beginning of the seven-year period, *if* Christians were still here at that time, we could instantly identify the Antichrist. We would not have to wait until the middle of the seven-year period to find out his identity.

The revealing of the Antichrist is at the *beginning* of the Daniel's seventieth week!

The Birth Pangs

In Matthew 24, the disciples asked Jesus the question: What was the sign of the end of the age? The phrases "end of the age" and the "time of the end" are found in the book of Daniel.

> "And some of them of understanding shall fall, to try them, and to purge, and to make them white, even to the time of the end: because it is yet for a time appointed." *Daniel 11:35*

In Daniel 7:24-25 we learn that there are ten nations that will arise at the time of the end, perhaps as a coalition. When the Antichrist starts to enforce the covenant, three of the ten nations will rebel against him. Daniel then details the spectacular rise of the Antichrist. Here in verse 40, he wrote that this will include the war the Antichrist fights against Egypt. Egypt is one of the three countries that will rebel against the Antichrist in his rise to power.

> "And at the time of the end shall the king of the south push at him: and the king of the north shall come against him like a whirlwind, with chariots, and with horsemen, and with many ships; and he shall enter into the countries, and shall overflow and pass over." *Daniel 11:40*

Daniel clearly shows in these two verses, that the phrase "time of the end" is synonymous with the seven-year period described in Daniel 9:27.

Jesus said before the time of the final "end" of the age, a series of things would happen. Jesus calls these events the "birth pangs." When a pregnant woman starts having labor pains five minutes apart, you know the birth is about to occur. Likewise, when you see these events take place, the time of the end, the seven-year period, is about to materialize. Jesus describes the birth pangs as:

"...the disciples came unto Him privately, saying, Tell us, when shall these things be? and what shall be the sign of Thy coming, and of the end of the world? [4]And Jesus answered and said unto them, Take heed that no man deceive you. [5]For many shall come in My name, saying, I am Christ; and shall deceive many. [6]And ye shall hear of wars and rumours of wars: see that ye be not troubled: for all these things must come to pass, but the end is not yet." *Matthew 24:3-6*

Jesus says the first thing to look for is people rising up and saying they are "Christ." In the chapter on the apostasy, we will see that the ancient church fathers taught this included the idea of a "Christ consciousness" being taught from within the church itself! Jesus listed a series of events to look for before the time of the end.

"[7]For nation shall rise against nation, and kingdom against kingdom: and there shall be famines, and pestilences, and earthquakes, in divers places. [8]All these are the beginning of sorrows [birth pangs]. [9]Then shall

The Birthpangs	
False Christs will appear	V. 5
Rumors of wars	V. 6
Famines and pestilences	V. 7
Earthquakes	V. 7
All nations will hate believers	V. 9
Many fall away from the faith	V. 10
Discord among churches	V. 10
False prophets arise	V. 11
Sin will increase	V. 12
The love of many will wax cold	V. 12
Gospel preached to all nations	V. 14

they deliver you up to be afflicted, and shall kill you: and ye shall be hated of all nations for My name's sake. [10]And then shall many be offended, and shall betray one another, and shall hate one another. [11]And many false prophets shall rise, and shall deceive many. [12]And because iniquity shall abound, the love

43

The Rapture

of many shall wax cold. [13]But he that shall endure unto the end, the same shall be saved. [14]And this gospel of the kingdom shall be preached in all the world for a witness unto all nations; and then shall the end come." *Matthew 24:7-14*

In this chapter we want to deal only with the events before the seven-year period. The rest of Jesus' predictions will be examined in the next chapter.

Obadiah – Before the Day of the Lord
Obadiah speaks mainly about the ancient wars between Israel and Edom. Edom is now present-day Jordan. Obadiah gives us a few prophecies that will occur right as the Day of the Lord is approaching. This is during the time of the birth pangs.

"For the day of the LORD draws near… Then those of the Negev will possess the mountain of Esau, And those of the Shephelah the Philistine plain; Also, possess the territory of Ephraim and the territory of Samaria," *Obadiah15, 19a-21 NASB*

These prophecies were fulfilled in 1948, when Israel was declared a nation and the Muslims that lived in the central and southern parts of Israel fled to the Gaza strip (the Philistine plain), Jordan (the mount of Esau), and Samaria (the West Bank).

Obadiah continues to prophesy of a yet-to-be-fulfilled war, one in which the Israelis will take and hold southern Lebanon up to modern Sarafand, Lebanon. In ancient times Sarafand was called Zaraphath. According to the prophecy, a remnant from the tribe of Benjamin will be found and migrate to Israel. They will settle in ancient Gilead (the most northern part of modern Jordan). History records that a large number of Jews left Jerusalem right before Titus destroyed the Temple. They settled in Sepharad, which is the Hebrew word for the country of Spain. Their descendants will migrate back to the land and colonize the Negev desert. Large portions of the Negev have not been colonized because of a lack of fresh water. Apparently, this problem will be overcome in the very near future.

"And Benjamin will possess Gilead. And the exiles of this host of the sons of Israel, Who are among the Canaanites as far as Zarephath, And the exiles of Jerusalem who are in Sepharad Will possess the cities of the Negev." *Obadiah19b-20 NASB*

The West Bank Becomes a Sovereign State
Daniel 11:45 predicts this area of the West Bank will be the place the Antichrist selects for his international headquarters before he invades Israel.

"He will pitch the tents of his royal pavilion between the seas and the beautiful Holy Mountain; yet he will come to his end, and no one will help him." *Daniel 11:45 NASB*

The "Holy Mountain" is Mount Moriah, where the Israeli city of Jerusalem sets. The "two seas" are the Mediterranean Sea and the Sea of Galilee. The land that these three locations surround is the West Bank. Therefore, sometime during the birth pangs, the West Bank must become an independent sovereign state. Presently, I have no idea what it will be named.

Ten Nations Arise
Daniel describes ten nations coming together to form a new world order. Each of the ten nations will be nations that were part of the old Roman Empire that fell in AD 476. See *Ancient Prophecies Revealed* for a complete study of these ten nations.

The Rapture

"And the ten horns out of this kingdom are ten kings that shall arise: and another shall rise after them; and he shall be diverse from the first, and he shall subdue three kings." *Daniel 7:24*

The Antichrist peacefully becomes the ruler of the ten nations and afterwards destroys three that rebel against him. Egypt will be one of those three nations. Since these facts are true, the ten nations must arise before the Antichrist comes on the scene, during the time of the birth pangs.

Birth Pangs of the Messiah

In the Jewish Talmud, Sanhedrin 97b, there is a list of ten signs called the Birth Pangs of the Messiah. Modern rabbis admit they don't know why the signs are called the Birth Pangs of the Messiah. Christians understand they refer to events leading up to the time that the whole nation of Israel will be "birthed into" Messiah. In other words, they are the signs that occur before the Second Coming of Jesus Christ. The signs are:

1. The Jews will return to their biblical homeland and the desert will bloom.
2. The world will be in a state of complete degradation.
3. Truth will decrease and lies will prevail.
4. Inflation will be out of control.
5. There will be fewer and fewer wise and righteous people.
6. Many Jews will give up the hope of redemption.
7. The young will treat the old with disrespect.
8. Learning will be rejected because people will desire a life of ease.
9. The whole world will turn against Israel.
10. The Jews will fight each other (the secular against the religious).

46

The Talmud also adds that God will defeat Israel's enemies in the war of Gog and Magog (Ezekiel 38 and 39) and confirm the nation of Israel is God's chosen people.

Ancient Prophecies Revealed
The knowledge of God and the understanding of prophecies will increase in the last days. See Daniel 12:4 and Isaiah 11:9. The more prophecies we see fulfilled, the more we will understand about all of them as a whole.

> "But as for you, Daniel, conceal these words and seal up the book until the end of time; many will go back and forth, and knowledge will increase."
> *Daniel 12:4 NASB*

Ancient church father Irenaeus understood Daniel to mean that after the second return of the Jewish people to Israel, all the prophecies would begin to be understood. His version of Daniel 12:4 reads this way:

> "Daniel the prophet says 'Shut up the words, and seal the book even to the time of consummation, until many learn, and knowledge be completed. For at that time, when the dispersion shall be accomplished, they shall know all these things.'"
> *Irenaeus, Against Heresies 4.26*

In the book *Ancient Prophecies Revealed,* we list more than thirty prophecies fulfilled during the early days of the church and the Middle Ages up to the time of the return of the nation of Israel in AD 1948. We then list fifty-three prophecies fulfilled since Israel became a state and the present time, AD 1948-2008. There are another fifteen prophecies to be fulfilled between 2008 and the beginning of the seven-year period. After that, the book lists, in chronological order, more than eighty prophecies about the Antichrist and the seven-year tribulation. It finishes with

The Rapture
more than twenty prophecies about the millennial reign of
Jesus Christ.

Now we need to discuss the "falling away" or "apostasy"
which completely manifests during the time of the birth
pangs.

The Apostasy

Paul warns in 2 Thessalonians 2:3 that the apostasy will come before the Antichrist is revealed. In this chapter we will define exactly what an apostasy is, so we know what to look for.

The word "apostasy" means to leave your faith for another belief. When the apostle Paul converted to Christianity, Acts 21 records the Jews called him an apostate from the Law of Moses. The Greek word "apostasia" is the word used for "the apostasy" in 2 Thessalonians 2:3 and is the same Greek word used for "forsake" in Acts 21:21.

> "And they are informed of thee, that thou teachest all the Jews which are among the Gentiles to forsake Moses, saying that they ought not to circumcise their children, neither to walk after the customs."
> *Acts 21:21*

With this in mind, do the Scriptures teach the end time church will apostatize; and if so, what signs do we look for? Revelation chapter 18 describes an end time church called the harlot church. So, the answer to our first question – is there an apostasy of the church? is yes! That apostate church will be the harlot church. These church members will think they are Christians but will have deviated so far away from the teaching of the Scriptures that they are not even truly saved. They are on their way to hell.

Doctrines of Demons

Paul defines the apostasy as departing from the true faith and accepting demonic doctrines.

> "Now the Spirit speaketh expressly, that in the latter times some shall depart from the faith, giving heed to

> seducing spirits, and doctrines of devils; Speaking lies in hypocrisy; having their conscience seared with a hot iron; *1 Timothy 4:1-2*

Paul continues to explain that two of those demonic doctrines are forbidding people to marry and to eat meat.

> "Forbidding to marry, and commanding to abstain from meats, which God hath created to be received with thanksgiving of them which believe and know the truth." *1 Timothy 4:3*

To identify the apostasy, we need to list the most important false teachings that it will include. We will list these point by point from Scripture.

Prophecy, Inspiration, and Evolution
The apostle Peter predicted scoffers would arise in the last days. These men would deny the inspiration of Scripture. They would reject the creation account in the book of Genesis and accept the Hindu doctrine of evolution. They would also reject the premillennial view of the return of Christ and despise prophecy in general.

> "Knowing this first, that there shall come in the last days scoffers, walking after their own lusts, And saying, Where is the promise of his coming? for since the fathers fell asleep, all things continue as they were from the beginning of the creation. For this they willingly are ignorant of, that by the word of God the heavens were of old, and the earth standing out of the water and in the water: Whereby the world that then was, being overflowed with water, perished: But the heavens and the earth, which are now, by the same word are kept in store, reserved unto fire against the day of judgment and perdition of ungodly men... But the day of the Lord will come as a thief in the night;

in the which the heavens shall pass away with a great
noise, and the elements shall melt with fervent heat,
the earth also and the works that are therein shall be
burned up." *2 Peter 3:3-7,10*

Mantras and Meditation
In Matthew 6:7, Jesus said not to pray like the heathen do,
using "vain repetitions." In practice, this is done using
mantras. A mantra is a word or phrase repeated over and
over until one enters an altered state of consciousness.
People also enter an altered state of consciousness by using
breathing techniques, also called "breath prayers." Any form
of eastern meditation that creates an altered state of
consciousness constitutes praying like the heathen do.

"And when you are praying, do not use meaningless
repetition as the Gentiles do, for they suppose that
they will be heard for their many words."
Matthew 6:7 NASB

Denial of the Doctrine of Christ
Peter prophesied that false prophets would rise up in the
church and deny the "master that bought them." Jesus is our
master and to deny Him means to deny what He is and what
He did. The first and second epistles of John teach the
Doctrine of Christ. This is what you must believe about Jesus
in order to be a Christian. In the end times the church will
deny these:

"But there were false prophets also among the people,
even as there shall be false teachers among you, who
privily shall bring in damnable heresies, even denying
the Lord that bought them, and bring upon themselves
swift destruction." *2 Peter 2:1*

The Rapture
The following chart lists the doctrines about Jesus Christ that the Antichrist will deny. These are essential doctrines every real Christian will believe.

Doctrine of Christ
1. Jesus is the one and only Christ. (1 Jn 2:22)
2. Jesus is from the beginning, eternal. (1 Jn 2:13; Mic 5:2)
3. Jesus had no sin. (1 Jn 3:5)
4. Jesus came in the flesh. (Jn 1:14; 1 Jn 4:2; 5:1,5; 2 Jn 7)
5. He resurrected in the flesh. (Jn 20:26-29; Lk 24:39)
6. Jesus is the Son of God. (1 Jn 5:1,5)
7. Jesus will come back in the flesh. (2 Jn 7; Acts 1:9-11)
8. Jesus is the one and only begotten Son of God. (1 Jn 4:15)
9. Jesus is God incarnate. (Jn 1:1-3; 5:17-18; 8:24; 8:56-59; 10:30-33; 20:26-29)

In the mind of the apostle John, denying that Jesus was the one and only Christ was quite possibly the worst thing anyone could do.

> "Who is a liar but he that denieth that Jesus is the Christ? He is antichrist, that denieth the Father and the Son." *1 John 2:22*

Jesus describes the birth pangs as the time between the rebirth of Israel in 1948 and the start of the seven-year period. During this time the only doctrinal sign that Jesus mentions is that many will come saying they are Christ.

> "For many shall come in my name, saying, I am Christ; and shall deceive many." *Matthew 24:5*

It does not say many will say "I am Jesus," so this does not mean they are teaching they are the reincarnation of Jesus Christ. They say, "I am Christ." They mean by this that they have "the Christ consciousness." This heresy was taught by many of the first century Gnostic cults.

Paul, in describing the apostasy, says that the mystery of iniquity is already at work. He is referring to the fact that this same concept of a Christ consciousness existed in his day.

Many of the ancient church fathers taught believing in a Christ consciousness was one of the ways people would come to believe they are a Christ in the last times. Today we see this in that New Age meditative kind of prayer that makes practitioners think they really are a god. This is called "sorcery" in the Old Testament and "the apostasy" by Paul in the New Testament. See the book *Ancient Paganism* for complete details on meditation and sorcery.

In 1 Timothy 1, Paul stated he excommunicated Alexander for blasphemy.

"This charge I commit unto thee, son Timothy, according to the prophecies which went before on thee, that thou by them mightest war a good warfare; Holding faith, and a good conscience; which some having put away concerning faith have made shipwreck: Of whom is Hymenaeus and Alexander; whom I have delivered unto Satan, that they may learn not to blaspheme." *1 Timothy 1:18-20*

What was *so* evil about Alexander's teaching that caused the apostle Paul to excommunicate him?

Tertullian wrote in chapter sixteen of his book *Flesh of Christ*, that Alexander left the true faith and joined a subgroup of the Ebionites who followed several heresies: that Jesus was just a man with a sin nature, that there is no physical resurrection and that people can become sinless by obtaining the Christ consciousness.

The Rapture

So, we have Jesus Christ, plus the apostles John and Paul clearly teaching that the apostasy will be based upon what we call the New Age idea of a Christ consciousness.

Conclusion

The main point I want point out in our study on the Rapture is that Jesus has the apostasy occurring during the birth pangs which takes place before the "time of the end of the age." Daniel 11 defines the time of the end as the whole seven-year period.

Likewise, the apostle Paul says the apostasy occurs *before* the "Day of the Lord," which we have seen is another term for the seven-year period.

What Jesus Said

Matthew 24 is commonly called the Olivette Discourse because Jesus explained end time events to His disciples while sitting on the Mount of Olives.

Jesus predicted the destruction of the temple in Matthew 24:1-2. Afterward His disciples asked Him:

> "Now as He sat on the Mount of Olives, the disciples came to Him privately, saying, 'Tell us, when will these things be? And what will be the sign of Your coming, and of the end of the age?'" *Matthew 24:3 NKJV*

The End of the Age

Jesus answered the question about the end of the age first. To properly interpret Jesus' end time instructions, we need to define the terms He used by linking them to the visions of the prophet Daniel. The term "end time" or the "time of the end" was used in Daniel to refer to the seven-year period.

Daniel 8:19 teaches the time of the end refers to the Antichrist's wars, the abomination, and the Antichrist's destruction. This "time of the end" is also called "the period of indignation."

Daniel 11:40 tells us this "time of the end" includes Egypt attacking the Antichrist; therefore, it includes the first and last half of the seven-year period.

> "And at the time of the end shall the king of the south push at him: and the king of the north shall come against him like a whirlwind, with chariots, and with horsemen, and with many ships; and he shall enter

into the countries, and shall overflow and pass over."
Daniel 11:40

In Daniel 12, Michael stands up "at that time" which refers back to the time of the end in Daniel 11. Just prior to the beginning of the seven-year period, the Rapture and Resurrection occur.

When Daniel asked about the timing of those events, the unnamed speaker told him there would be three and a half years between the beginning of the seven-year period and the time when the Antichrist starts the great persecution that "scatters the power of the holy people."

> "And I heard the man clothed in linen, which was upon the waters of the river, when he held up his right hand and his left hand unto heaven, and sware by him that liveth forever that it shall be for a time, times, and an half; and when he shall have accomplished to scatter the power of the holy people, all these things shall be finished." *Daniel 12:7*

Then Daniel asked another question and was told there would be 1290 days from the time of the setting up of the abomination of desolation, which starts "the scattering," to the end of the seven years.

> "And from the time that the daily sacrifice shall be taken away, and the abomination that maketh desolate set up, there shall be a thousand two hundred and ninety days." *Daniel 12:11*

So, Daniel 12 also clearly shows the "time of the end" is the seven-year period.
Using these verses, we can see the birth pangs are *before* the seven-year period, and the "time of the end of the age" refers to the seven-year period itself.

Birth Pangs

In Matthew 24:4-14, Jesus responded to the disciples' questions by saying there would be a series of events that will occur during the time of the birth pangs (called sorrows in the KJV). The birth pangs consist of the events right before the time of the end, or the seven-year period. After listing these things, Jesus said "then the end will come," referring back to the question in verse 3 about the "end of the age."

The Seven-Year Period

In verses 15-20, Jesus describes the time of the end. The abomination of desolation, which occurs in the *middle* of the seven-year tribulation, is set up.

In verses 21-22, Jesus teaches how the Antichrist starts the most severe persecution (Great Tribulation in the KJV) that has ever been. Jesus says unless *those days* are cut short no flesh would survive.

The Seventieth Week

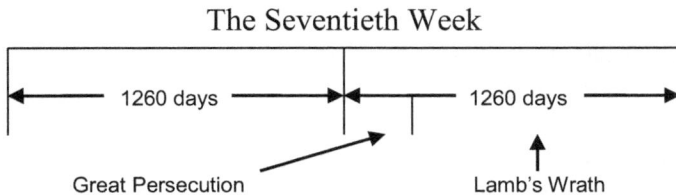

Jesus continued saying in verses 28-31, that immediately *after* that great persecution of the Antichrist reaches its height, the sun goes dark, which marks the *start* of the wrath of the Lamb during the *last half* of the seven-year tribulation period, according to Joel and Revelation. Jesus actually quoted Joel 2:31 and 3:15 in this passage.

After this Jesus will pour out His judgment and then the sign of the Son of Man will appear. This is a quote from Daniel

The Rapture
7:13. Daniel described this sign as when the Son of Man comes to destroy the Antichrist, (or beast) as Daniel calls him.

The Gathering at the Return

When the Lord returns, He will finish the Wrath with the Battle of Armageddon. Then "the gathering" is mentioned. This is where the raptured saints come back to earth, the martyred saints are resurrected, and the remaining saints are gathered from all over earth – all gathered to Israel.

> "And He shall send His angels with a great sound of a trumpet, and they shall gather together His elect from the four winds, from one end of heaven to the other." *Matthew 24:31*

> "And then shall He send His angels, and shall gather together His elect from the four winds, from the uttermost part of the earth to the uttermost part of heaven." *Mark 13:27*

Revelation 20 also states the Lord will resurrect martyred believers at this time.

> "And I saw thrones, and they sat upon them, and judgment was given unto them: and I saw the souls of them that were beheaded for the witness of Jesus, and for the word of God, and which had not worshipped the beast, neither his image, neither had received his mark upon their foreheads, or in their hands; and they lived and reigned with Christ a thousand years." *Revelation 20:4*

After all this the great trump is blown (see the chapter on rabbinic festivals for details) and His elect are gathered from heaven back to earth. This finishes the Second Coming. The

Great Trump is a name for the festival of Yom Kippur which teaches about the Second Coming.

The Coming of Jesus
After Jesus finished describing the signs of the birth pangs and time of the end, He answered the other question put to Him in verse 3: "When shall these things be?" His answer seems a bit cryptic. He told the disciples, in verse 32, to learn the parable of the fig tree.

"Now learn a parable of the fig tree; When his branch is yet tender, and putteth forth leaves, ye know that summer is nigh: So likewise, ye, when ye shall see all these things, know that it is near, even at the doors."
Matthew 24:32-33

Jesus meant when you see these things begin, you know the rest will soon follow. The fig tree has always been a symbol of the nation of Israel in the Old Testament. This being the case, Jesus could be saying when you see the budding or return of the nation of Israel, which occurred in 1948 AD, you should know that the time of the birth pangs has begun!

The Day and Hour
No one will know the day or hour of the next coming of Jesus. If you see the revealing of the Antichrist, which will occur when he sends in his troops to enforce the peace plan, and Egypt responds by attacking him; you will also know that in 1260 days the abomination of desolation will be set up in the temple. From the time of the abomination of desolation to the return of Jesus to set up His kingdom will be another 1260 days. The only part of the Day of the Lord you will never know until it happens is the start: the Resurrection and Rapture.

"But of that day and hour knoweth no man, no, not the angels of heaven, but my Father only. But as the

The Rapture

days of Noe were, so shall also the coming of the Son of man be. For as in the days that were before the flood they were eating and drinking, marrying and giving in marriage, until the day that Noe entered into the ark, And knew not until the flood came, and took them all away; so shall also the coming of the Son of man be." *Matthew 24:36-39*

After this passage, Jesus continued to describe what the first part of His coming will be like. He describes the Rapture!

"Then shall two be in the field; the one shall be taken, and the other left. Two women shall be grinding at the mill; the one shall be taken, and the other left. Watch therefore: for ye know not what hour your Lord doth come." *Matthew 24:40-42*

Based on these prophecies, we will know when the Second Coming will happen and when the abomination will be set up. So, if there is a posttribulational or a midtribulational rapture, we would also know the date of the Rapture before it happens, and these verses would be a lie!

You can't say Jesus meant they didn't know the date of the prophecies in His day but might figure them out after the New Testament was written; because they all knew the prophecies of Daniel. So, they had these dates in writing back then.

Luke's Version
Luke states just as Noah was taken out of the way before the world was destroyed and just like Lot was taken out of the way before Sodom was destroyed, so it shall be when Jesus returns. First the true believers will be raptured, then the day of the Lord will begin.

60

"And as it was in the days of Noe, so shall it be also in the days of the Son of man. They did eat, they drank, they married wives, they were given in marriage, until the day that Noah entered into the ark, and the flood came, and destroyed them all. Likewise also as it was in the days of Lot; they did eat, they drank, they bought, they sold, they planted, they builded; But the same day that Lot went out of Sodom it rained fire and brimstone from heaven, and destroyed them all. Even thus shall it be in the day when the Son of man is revealed. In that day, he which shall be upon the housetop, and his stuff in the house, let him not come down to take it away: and he that is in the field, let him likewise not return back. Remember Lot's wife. Whosoever shall seek to save his life shall lose it; and whosoever shall lose his life shall preserve it. I tell you, in that night there shall be two men in one bed; the one shall be taken, and the other shall be left. Two women shall be grinding together; the one shall be taken, and the other left. Two men shall be in the field; the one shall be taken, and the other left. And they answered and said unto Him, Where, Lord? And He said unto them, Wheresoever the body is, thither will the eagles be gathered together." *Luke 17:26-37*

Jesus instructs that when you see the birth pangs, take heed so that "that day" not come upon you unawares, or like a thief. Pray that you are counted worthy to escape (in the Rapture).

This overtaking or "snare" will come upon "all who dwell upon the whole earth." The only way to escape is to be raptured off the earth and stand before the Son of Man at the Bema judgment seat of Christ.

The Rapture

Second Thessalonians states that that day overtakes many "like a thief" when sudden destruction comes upon them. The destruction will not overtake Christians like a thief because we are not subject to the wrath of God. We are raptured out.

"And take heed to yourselves, lest at any time your hearts be overcharged with surfeiting, and drunkenness, and cares of this life, and so that day come upon you unawares. For as a snare shall it come on all them that dwell on the face of the whole earth. Watch ye therefore, and pray always, that ye may be accounted worthy to escape all these things that shall come to pass, and to stand before the Son of man." *Luke 21:34-36*

Conclusion

Notice the sequence. The doctrinal part of the birth pangs is a belief in the New Age doctrine of the Christ consciousness. This is an apostasy from faith. So, the apostasy occurs *before* the time of the end. We have proven clearly the time of the end is the whole seven-year period. Jesus said in the parable of the fig tree that the time of the end (or the seven-year period) will start with some people being caught up.

This is the same order that Paul gives in 2 Thessalonians 2, which we will see in the next chapter.

The Pretribulational Rapture
1 and 2 Thessalonians

In the first chapter we looked at the definition of the Rapture of the church from 1 Thessalonians 4.

> "For this we say unto you by the word of the Lord, that we which are alive and remain unto the coming of the Lord shall not prevent them which are asleep. For the Lord Himself shall descend from heaven with a shout, with the voice of the archangel, and with the trump of God: and the dead in Christ shall rise first: Then we which are alive and remain shall be caught up together with them in the clouds, to meet the Lord in the air: and so shall we ever be with the Lord. Wherefore comfort one another with these words."
> *1 Thessalonians 4:15-18*

After Paul defined the Rapture, he connected it with the "Day of the Lord." We have proven from the prophecies of Amos 5, Daniel 11, and Revelation 6 that the "Day of the Lord" is the seven-year period. The destruction comes upon the unbelievers suddenly and unexpectedly.

> "But of the times and the seasons, brethren, ye have no need that I write unto you. For yourselves know perfectly that the day of the Lord so cometh as a thief in the night. For when they shall say, Peace and safety; then sudden destruction cometh upon them, as travail upon a woman with child; and they shall not escape." *1 Thessalonians 5:1-3*

Notice Paul also connected this with Jesus' Matthew 24 teaching about the time of the end, or the seven-year period, coming as a thief. The sudden destruction does not come upon the Christians because they "escape" in the Rapture.

63

The Rapture

> "But ye, brethren, are not in darkness, that that day should overtake you as a thief. Ye are all the children of light, and the children of the day: we are not of the night, nor of darkness. Therefore, let us not sleep, as do others; but let us watch and be sober. For they that sleep sleep in the night; and they that be drunken are drunken in the night. But let us, who are of the day, be sober, putting on the breastplate of faith and love; and for an helmet, the hope of salvation."
> *1 Thessalonians 5:4-8*

Paul concludes the discussion on the Rapture and the Day of the Lord by saying we should remember we are not appointed to "wrath," but to obtain salvation when those that sleep resurrect and those awake are changed. In other words, the "Day of Wrath" or the seven-year period will not hurt us because we obtain salvation through the Rapture.

> "For God hath not appointed us to wrath, but to obtain salvation by our Lord Jesus Christ, Who died for us, that, whether we wake or sleep, we should live together with Him. Wherefore comfort yourselves together, and edify one another, even as also ye do."
> *1 Thessalonians 5:9-11*

The Order of the Day of the Lord
With this in mind let's look at the order of the "Day of the Lord" that Paul gives in 2 Thessalonians 2.

> "Now we beseech you, brethren, by the coming of our Lord Jesus Christ, and by our gathering together unto Him," *2 Thessalonians 2:1*

Paul says the following information is in regard to "the coming" and "our being gathered to Him." Whether the Rapture is pre-, mid-, or post-tribulational, the very next time

Jesus "comes" He will "gather us" by the Rapture that Paul just defined in 1 Thessalonians 4 and 5.

Paul is saying in regard to the Rapture...

> "That ye be not soon shaken in mind, or be troubled, neither by spirit, nor by word, nor by letter as from us, as that the day of Christ is at hand."
> *2 Thessalonians 2:2*

In verse two, Paul says we should not be afraid that the Day of Christ has come. We know that that the phrase "Day of Christ" in this passage is the seven-year period commonly called the "Day of the Lord," because Paul goes on to describe the revealing of the Antichrist and his destruction which occur in that seven-year period.

> "Let no man deceive you by any means: for that day shall not come, except there come a falling away first, and that man of sin be revealed, the son of perdition;"
> *2 Thessalonians 2:3*

Paul makes sure we understand that the Day of the Lord will not start until the "falling away" occurs and the Antichrist is revealed. We have proven that the revealing of the Antichrist is at the beginning of the seven-year period and that the Day of the Lord is the seven-year period. We have also seen that Jesus taught the apostasy, or falling away, begins to manifest during the birth pangs, the time right before the start of the seven-year period.

> "Who opposeth and exalteth himself above all that is called God, or that is worshipped; so that he as God sitteth in the temple of God, shewing himself that he is God. Remember ye not, that, when I was yet with you, I told you these things?" *2 Thessalonians 2:4-5*

The Rapture
In verse 4, Paul is referring to the event recorded in Daniel 9. Daniel wrote that at the start of the seven-year period the Antichrist will be revealed when he confirms the covenant, and in the middle of the seven-years he causes the sacrifices in the Jerusalem temple to stop.   Daniel 11:36 and 2 Thessalonians 2:4 also agree that he will claim to be God incarnate.

> "And now ye know what withholdeth that he might be revealed in his time." *2 Thessalonians 2:6*

Paul says now you know what withholds "him." So, Paul has to be referring to the Antichrist, not the apostasy or the Day of the Lord. The event that withholds the revealing of the Antichrist is referenced in verse two: our being gathered unto Messiah at His next coming to earth.

> "For the mystery of iniquity doth already work: only He who now letteth will let, until He be taken out of the way.   And then shall that Wicked be revealed, whom the Lord shall consume with the spirit of His mouth, and shall destroy with the brightness of His coming:" *2 Thessalonians 2:7-8*

This apostasy or mystery of lawlessness was already at work in the form of the Gnostic cults invading the church even in Paul's day.

It Comes Out of the Midst
The Greek of verse seven literally says "only the one continues restraining, until out of the midst it comes."

The restrainer restrains the revealing of the Antichrist until the beginning of the seven-year period. The restrainer stops restraining when "it comes out of the midst." What is "it" and from the midst of "what" does it come? Four theories have been proposed. They are:

Pretribulational Rapture
1. The Day of the Lord coming from the midst of the church age
2. The apostasy fully forming at the end of the church age
3. The apostasy coming from the midst of the church age
4. The rapture of the church coming from the midst of the earth

From "the midst" means "from the middle" or "from inside of." This Greek phrase is never used in a sequence, such as the first, middle, and last. Both the Day of the Lord and the full manifestation of the Apostasy occur at the *end* of the church age. This means theories one and two can't be what Paul is referring to, because they do not come from within the church.

Paul does say the "mystery of lawlessness is already at work," so the beginnings of the apostasy started in the first century and have always been here throughout the church age. The apostasy does come from within the church itself. While the apostasy does come out of the church, this can't be what Paul is referring to either, because the mystery of lawlessness changes with the times. The form it will take in the end times will indeed come from within the church, but that is at the end of days. So, grammatically, theory number three does not fit, either.

The only conclusion we can come to is that Paul is referring to the church being raptured from the midst of the earth. We will see in the next chapter that some of the ancient church fathers taught this theory as well.

The idea behind Paul's use of the Greek word "apostasia" describes the church degrading into an apostate religion in the end times. A pre-tribulational rapture would remove the last bastion of true Christianity and allow the apostasy to become complete.

The Rapture

Back in verse one Paul says these things are in regard to the Rapture. So, Paul's thought is the Day of the Lord can't come until the Antichrist is revealed. That occurs immediately after the Rapture. The apostasy of the church will not be

Order of Events
The Apostasy
Antichrist Revealed
Antichrist in the Temple
Temple sacrifices stop
Jesus Returns
Antichrist destroyed

complete until the true believers are "gathered unto him" by the Rapture so that the unbelievers left behind can solidify all the denominations into one super apostate harlot church.

Love of the Truth

Paul writes in verses nine and ten that those who do not receive a love of the truth will fall for the Antichrist's lying signs and wonders. Those who don't have a love for the truth of God's Word and for the prophecies enough to study them seriously, will not even be aware of the prophecies and will fall for the lie.

> "Even him, whose coming is after the working of Satan with all power and signs and lying wonders, And with all deceivableness of unrighteousness in them that perish; because they received not the love of the truth, that they might be saved."
> *2 Thessalonians 2:9-10*

Jesus said these lying signs would be so deceptive that *if it were possible* the elect would fall for them. But since they have a love for the truth (they love to study the prophecies), they will not fall for the lie.

> "For there shall arise false christs, and false prophets, and shall shew great signs and wonders; insomuch that, if it were possible, they shall deceive the very elect." *Matthew 24:24*

Because they are *willingly* ignorant of the biblical prophecies, and of God in general, God sends them the delusion. This delusion causes them to no longer doubt the lie that the Antichrist is a god.

"And for this cause God shall send them strong delusion, that they should believe a lie: That they all might be damned who believed not the truth, but had pleasure in unrighteousness."
2 Thessalonians 2:11-12

Conclusion
When the true believers are taken out of the midst of the earth in the Rapture/gathering, *then* the deluding influence of the apostasy can take full effect and the Antichrist can be revealed. The apostasy is the sign that the restrainer is about to take the church "out of the midst" of the earth. The Scriptures also teach that the church will not be subject to the "wrath" of the seven-year Tribulation. Luke 21:23 says the "wrath" is for His people Israel. The church is not appointed to wrath, (1 Thessalonians 5:9) and will be kept from the hour of trial (Revelation 3:10) because the gates of hell will not prevail against the church (Matthew 16:18).

Rapture or Apostasy?

In the chapter entitled *The Apostasy*, we studied the apostasy of faith that would come before the Antichrist is revealed. All theologians agree that there will be an apostasy at this time, but some think that the Greek word "apostasia," (Strong's Greek #646) translated as "falling away," found in 2 Thessalonians 2, actually means "departure" and refers to the Rapture of the church. This word is used as a noun in two places in the New Testament. It is translated as "falling away" in 2 Thessalonians 2 and "forsake" in Acts 21.

> "Let no man deceive you by any means: for *that day shall not come,* except there come a <u>falling away</u> first, and that man of sin be revealed, the son of perdition"
> *2 Thessalonians 2:3*

> "And they are informed of thee, that thou teachest all the Jews which are among the Gentiles to <u>forsake</u> Moses, saying that they ought not to circumcise *their* children, neither to walk after the customs."
> *Acts 21:21*

In Acts Paul is being accused of departing (apostatizing) from the Hebrew religion, which is why most see 2 Thessalonians 2 as a departure from the faith. However, if we take into account the verb form of this same word, which is "aphistemi" (Strong's Greek #868), we find it occurs another sixteen times. Each time it only means departure, in the sense of leaving a room. Here are the sixteen references with "aphistemi" underlined in the verse.

"And she [Anna] *was* a widow of about fourscore and four years, which <u>departed</u> not from the temple, but served *God* with fastings and prayers night and day." *Luke 2:37*

"And when the devil had ended all the temptation, he <u>departed</u> from Him for a season." *Luke 4:13*

"They on the rock *are they,* which, when they hear, receive the word with joy; and these have no root, which for a while believe, and in time of temptation <u>fall away</u>." *Luke 8:13*

"But he shall say, I tell you, I know you not whence ye are; <u>depart</u> from me, all *ye* workers of iniquity." *Luke 13:27*

"After this man rose up Judas of Galilee in the days of the taxing, and <u>drew away</u> much people after him: he also perished; and all, *even* as many as obeyed him, were dispersed. And now I say unto you, <u>Refrain</u> from these men, and let them alone: for if this counsel or this work be of men, it will come to nought:" *Acts 5:37-38*

"[An angel broke Peter out of jail.] When they were past the first and the second ward, they came unto the iron gate that leadeth unto the city; which opened to them of his own accord: and they went out, and passed on through one street; and forthwith the angel <u>departed</u> from him." *Acts 12:10*

The Rapture

"But Paul thought not good to take him with them, who <u>departed</u> from them from Pamphylia, and went not with them to the work." *Acts 15:38*

"But when divers were hardened, and believed not, but spake evil of that way before the multitude, he <u>departed</u> from them, and separated the disciples, disputing daily in the school of one Tyrannus." *Acts 19:9*

"Then straightway they <u>departed</u> from him which should have examined him: and the chief captain also was afraid, after he knew that he was a Roman, and because he had bound him." *Acts 22:29*

"For this thing I besought the Lord thrice, that it might <u>depart</u> from me." *2 Corinthians 12:8*

"Now the Spirit speaketh expressly, that in the latter times some shall <u>depart</u> from the faith, giving heed to seducing spirits, and doctrines of devils" *1 Timothy 4:1*

"Perverse disputings of men of corrupt minds, and destitute of the truth, supposing that gain is godliness: from such <u>withdraw</u> thyself." *1 Timothy 6:5*

"Nevertheless, the foundation of God standeth sure, having this seal, The Lord knoweth them that are His. And, Let every one that nameth the name of Christ <u>depart</u> from iniquity." *2 Timothy 2:19*

"Take heed, brethren, lest there be in any of you an evil heart of unbelief, in <u>departing</u> from the living God." *Hebrews 3:12*

We learn from this study that an "apostasy" is simply a departure, sometimes from the faith and sometimes from other things. This doesn't prove that the apostasy spoken of in 2 Thessalonians 2 is the Rapture of the church, but it could refer to that.

All modern Bibles translate the word as apostasy, but were there ever any ancient translations that translated it as simply "departure"? Yes, and here are a few examples, starting with the KJV 1611 and going back:

1611, KJV, falling away
1608, Geneva Bible, departing
1583, Beeza Bible, departing
1582, Reims Bible, revolt
1576, Breeches Bible, departing
1539, Crammer Bible, departing
1535, Coverdale Bible, departynge
1526, Tyndale Bible, departynge
1384, Wycliffe Bible, departynge

So, in conclusion, 2 Thessalonians 2:7 may be stating that the Rapture must come first before the rise of the Antichrist, which fits with our understanding of a pretribulational Rapture. But the "departing" may be a departing from the faith, which also fits with the pretribulational Rapture.

Pretribulational Church Fathers

You may have heard that the teaching of a pretribulational Rapture was invented by James Darby in the 1800's. While it is true that Darby brought back the teaching and made it popular, it is not true that he was the first to teach the Rapture in this way.

The following is a list of pretribulationists from the ancient church. These men may or may not be correct in their theology, but they definitely show the pretribulational Rapture was a common belief in the ancient church.

Famous Pretribulationists
Shepherd of Hermas, AD 150
Irenaeus, AD 170
Hippolytus, AD 210
Victorinus, AD 240
Cyprian, AD 250
Ephraim the Syrian, AD 373

Shepherd ~ AD 150
The Shepherd of Hermas was written about AD 150. It describes a dream and gives the interpretation of it. The church (bride clothed in white) escapes the Great Tribulation because of the promise of the Lord. The Shepherd of Hermas *is not to be considered Scripture*, but it does show that many second century Christians believed in a pre-tribulational Rapture.

"Go therefore and declare to the Elect of the Lord His mighty deeds and say to them that this beast is a type of **the great tribulation** which is to come. If ye therefore prepare yourselves and with your whole heart turn to the Lord in repentance, then shall ye **be able to escape it**, if your heart is **pure and blameless**… the golden color stands for you who have escaped from this world… Now ye know the symbol of the **great tribulation** to come. But **if ye are willing, it shall be nothing**." *Shepard AD 150*

Irenaeus

Church father Irenaeus wrote in the mid-second century. He was taught under Polycarp, the disciple of the apostle John, and occasionally saw the apostle John. Irenaeus wrote a five-volume work entitled *Against Heresies* against the cults of his day. In this work he described the rapture of the church as pre-tribulational, refuting those who said there will be no physical resurrection. The church will be caught up, or raptured, *then* the seven-year tribulation will occur.

"When in the end that church will suddenly be caught up from this, then it is said, 'There will be tribulation such as not been since the beginning, nor will be.'" Irenaeus' *Against Heresies 5.29*

Hippolytus

Hippolytus was a disciple of Irenaeus, who wrote his own work against the cults of his day much like his spiritual father did before him. Hippolytus also wrote two works on prophecy, *On the Antichrist* and *On the End of the World*. In *On the Antichrist*, he called the Rapture our "blessed hope."

"These things, then, I have set shortly before you, Theophilus, drawing them from Scripture itself, in order that, maintaining in faith what is written, and anticipating the things that are to be, you may keep yourself void of offence both toward God and toward men, 'looking for that blessed hope and appearing of our God and Savior,' when, having raised the saints among us, He will rejoice with them, glorifying the Father. To Him be the glory unto the endless ages of the ages. Amen." Hippolytus' *On the Antichrist 67*

The Rapture

He then teaches, in *On the Antichrist*, that the quote from Isaiah 26:20 of our being "hidden" until the "indignation" is over refers to the time of the End that Paul taught of in Romans 1:18. Hippolytus believed our "blessed hope" was the Rapture before the coming of that seven-year tribulation.

> "By the heat he means the conflagration. And Isaiah speaks thus: 'Come, my people, enter thou into thy chamber, and shut thy door: hide thyself as it were for a little moment, until the indignation of the Lord be overpast.' And Paul in like manner: 'For the wrath of God is revealed from heaven against all ungodliness and unrighteousness of men, who hold the truth of God in unrighteousness.'"
> Hippolytus' *On the Antichrist 64b*

Hippolytus continues that line of reasoning saying those who hear the sound of the trumpet (Rapture /Resurrection) stand before the Lord at His coming and then the wrath is poured out. So, they do not resurrect after the wrath is poured out (post-trib Rapture theory) but before it begins.

We have already shown that the church fathers considered the whole seven-year period to be the time of "the Wrath." God uses the Antichrist's wrath in the first half then pours out His direct wrath in the second half.

> "For at that time the trumpet shall sound [1 Thess. 4:16] and awake those that sleep from the lowest parts of the earth, righteous and sinners alike. And every kindred, and tongue, and nation, and tribe shall be raised in the twinkling of an eye [1 Cor. 15:52]; and they shall stand upon the face of the earth, waiting for

the coming of the righteous and terrible Judge, in fear and trembling unutterable. For the river of fire shall come forth in fury like an angry sea, and shall burn up mountains and hills, and shall make the sea vanish, and shall dissolve the atmosphere with its heat like wax [2 Pet. 3:12]. The stars of heaven shall fall [Matt. 24:29], the sun shall be turned into darkness, and the moon into blood [Acts 2:20]. The heaven shall be rolled together like a scroll [Rev. 6:14]: the whole earth shall be burnt up by reason of the deeds done in it, which men did corruptly, in fornications, in adulteries, and in lies and uncleanness, and in idolatries, and in murders, and in battles. For there shall be the new heaven and the new earth [Rev. 21:1]." Hippolytus' *On the End of the World 37*

Victorinus ~ AD 240

One pretribulationist, Victorinus, wrote a commentary about AD 240 on the book of Revelation. In his commentary, Victorinus refers to Paul's phrase "only the one continues restraining, until out of the midst it comes." Victorinus clearly shows that he thinks it is the raptured church that has "gone out of the midst" of the earth.

"And I saw another great and wonderful sign, seven angels having the seven last plagues; for in them is completed the Wrath of God. (Revelation 15:1) and these shall be in the last time, when the *Church shall have gone out of the midst*." (2 Thessalonians 2:7)
Commentary on the Apocalypse 15.1 - Victorinus AD 240

Victorinus is saying that by the last time, or "time of the end," the church has already been taken away. In another place Victorinus shows he believes in a rapture of the church.

The Rapture
"The sky being split apart like a scroll is the *church being taken away.*" (Revelation 6:14)
Victorinus Commentary on Revelation 6:14 - AD 240

Cyprian ~ AD 250

Cyprian was the bishop of Carthage about AD 250. Notice he did not teach we must endure the time of the Antichrist, but we will be "delivered" from it. He told his readers that the coming resurrection was the hope of the Christian and pointed out that the Rapture "snatching us" should motivate us as we see the last days approaching.

"we who see that terrible things have begun, and know that still more terrible things are imminent, may regard it as the **greatest advantage to depart** from it as quickly as possible. Do you not give God thanks, do you not congratulate yourself, that by an **early departure you are taken away, and delivered** from the shipwrecks and disasters that are imminent? Let us greet the day which assigns each of us to his own home, which **snatches us hence**, and sets us free from the snares of the world, and **restores** us to paradise and the kingdom."
Treatises *of Cyprian – 21 to 26*

"The Antichrist is coming, but above him comes Christ also. The enemy goes about and rages, but immediately the Lord follows to avenge our suffering and our wounds. The adversary is enraged and threatens, but there is One who can **deliver us** from his hands." *Epistle 55 – Cyprian AD 250*

Ephraim ~ AD 373

This next quote is from a work entitled pseudo-Ephraim. It has the title pseudo, not because anyone doubted the sermon, but because when quoted later, two historians said it was Ephraim the Syrian who wrote it, and one historian said it

Pretribulational First Century Church was Isadore of Seville. Whether this was written by Isadore or Ephraim, the sermon has always been accepted as genuine. It clearly teaches the Rapture occurs before the seven-year Tribulation period.

> "...because all saints and the elect of the LORD are gathered together **before the Tribulation** which is about to come and be taken to the LORD..."
> *On the Last Times 2 – Ephraim the Syrian AD 373*

Middle Ages

These are some of the church fathers from the most ancient times. When premillennialism was replaced by amillennialism in the fourth century, the teaching of the Rapture itself (not to mention its timing) was ignored. When revival hit Europe with Luther, the Calvinists, and eventually Protestants, the teaching was revived because it was the teaching of the ancient church.

The Rapture in the Seventeenth Century

There are so many references we could cite, but in the interest of brevity we will list the Christian authors in groups as to what they taught about the Rapture.

Words used for the Rapture

Some authors used the word "Rapt" to mean the Rapture:

Vernon Manuscript, 1320s; John Lygate, 1420; William Bond, 1531; Thomas Draxe, 1613; Barton Holyday, 1626; Joseph Hall, 1635; George Walker, 1638; William Sherwin, 1665

Some authors used the word "Rapture" to mean the Rapture:

The Rapture

Barton Holyday, 1626; Joseph Mede, 1627; Nathaniel Homes, 1653; Capt. John Browne, 1654; William Sherwin, 1665-1700; Increase Mather, 1726; John Norris, 1738; Philip Doddridge, 1739; John Gill, 1748

Some authors did not use any word for the rapture but often taught the concept and used the phrase "left behind":

Robert Maton, 1642; Thomas Vincent, 1667; the author of *Theopolis*, 1672; Oliver Heywood, 1700; Thomas Pyle, 1715; Grantham Killingworth, 1761

Some authors taught that the Rapture/ Resurrection will occur *well before* the Second Coming:

William Bridge, 1641; Robert Maton, 1642; John Archer, 1642; Ephraim Huit (Huwitt), 1643; Samuel Hutchinson, 1646; Nathaniel Homes, 1653; Capt. John Brown, 1658; James Duram, 1658; John Birchensha, 1660; William Sherwin, 1665; William Hook, 1653; T.M.? 1680; John Mason, 1691; Jane Leade, 1702; John Floyer, 1721

The Rapture happens for the *safety* of those on the earth, to "escape the wrath":

Robert Maton, 1642; Jeremiah Burroughs, 1643; Ephraim Hewitt, 1643; Samuel Hutchinson, 1646; Elizabeth Avery 1647; Peter Sterry, 1648; Nathaniel Homes, 1653; John Apsinwall, 1653; Capt. John Browne, 1654; Archbishop Ussher, 1655; John Birchensha, 1660; Praisegod Barbones, 1675; T.M., 1680; M. Marsin, 1701; John Hildrop, 1711

80

Pretribulational First Century Church
Now let's look at some Old Testament passages that teach about the Rapture of believers in the last days.

The Rapture in the Old Testament

There are many Old Testament verses that indicate a pretribulational Rapture. Here are just a few:

Isaiah On the Rapture:
The prophet Isaiah spoke of the time right before the time of the Lord's Indignation (also called the Day of Indignation), when His people would be hidden in their bridal chamber. The church is always referred to as the bride of Christ. The Rapture/Resurrection occurs before the wrath is poured out. Notice the sequence of events: first the Resurrection, then the Rapture, then God's punishment.

> "Thy dead men shall live, together with my dead body shall they arise. Awake and sing, ye that dwell in dust: for thy dew is as the dew of herbs, and the earth shall cast out the dead. Come, my people, enter thou into thy chambers [chedar, or wedding chamber], and shut thy doors about thee: hide thyself as it were for a little moment, until the indignation be overpast. For, behold, the LORD cometh out of His place to punish the inhabitants of the earth for their iniquity: the earth also shall disclose her blood, and shall no more cover her slain." *Isaiah 26:19-21*

Removal Of the Gift of Tongues a Sign of the Rapture
Paul quotes Isaiah 28:11 in 1 Corinthians 14:21. Paul interprets this as a prophecy that the gift of speaking in tongues by the Christians is a sign that the nation of Israel, which had corporately rejected Jesus Christ as Messiah, was about to be destroyed.

> "For with stammering lips and another tongue will he speak to this people." *Isaiah 28:11*

"In the law it is written, With men of other tongues
and other lips will I speak unto this people; and yet
for all that will they not hear Me, saith the Lord."
1 Corinthians 14:21

Within forty years Jerusalem was destroyed by the Romans.
These same Hebrew phrases "stammering lips" and "another
tongue" are used in Isaiah 33. This prophecy states those in
the tribulation will no longer see the church, those who speak
in tongues. It asks, "where did they go?" They went to a far
distant land with the King of beauty; while they are gone the
people who remain, will be in terror. But when the appointed
feast is fulfilled, those who survive will see the King and the
church return.

"Your eyes will see the King in His beauty; they will
behold a far-distant land. Your heart will meditate on
terror: 'Where is he who counts? Where is he who
weighs? Where is he who counts the towers?' You
will no longer see a fierce people, a people of
unintelligible speech which no one comprehends, of a
stammering tongue which no one understands. Look
upon Zion, the city of our appointed feasts; your eyes
will see Jerusalem, an undisturbed habitation, a tent
which will not be folded; its stakes will never be
pulled up, nor any of its cords be torn apart."
Isaiah 33:17-20

The apostle Paul said the same thing in 1 Corinthians. Love
would continue forever, but prophecy would come to an end
when all prophecies are fulfilled. Tongues would not be seen
any longer when "that which is perfect comes."

"Charity never faileth: but whether there be
prophecies, they shall fail; whether there be tongues,
they shall cease; whether there be knowledge, it shall
vanish away. For we know in part, and we prophesy

The Rapture
in part. But when that which is perfect is come, then that which is in part shall be done away... For now we see through a glass darkly; but then face to face: now I know in part; but then shall I know even as also I am known." *1 Corinthians 13:8-10,12*

Ancient church father Irenaeus, in *Against Heresies 4.9*, stated that the spiritual gifts will continue to manifest in the church until "that which is perfect" has come and we see Him "face to face." In quoting these phrases from 1 Corinthians 13, Irenaeus taught the gifts would continue until the Rapture.

Zephaniah On the Rapture
Zechariah 9:1-8 prophesies that Ekron will be obliterated never to be restored, and Ashdod and Ashkelon will be taken over by a mixed race. This prediction was fulfilled by Alexander the Great. Zephaniah 2 gives the rest of the prophetical history. Zephaniah 2:4-6 explains that Alexander went on to destroy the nation of the Philistines. Ashdod and Ashkelon became desolate so that for centuries the countryside by the ocean was only used by shepherds and their flocks.

> "For Gaza shall be forsaken, and Ashkelon a desolation: they shall drive out Ashdod at the noon day, and Ekron shall be rooted up. Woe unto the inhabitants of the sea coast, the nation of the Cherethites! the word of the LORD is against you; O Canaan, the land of the Philistines, I will even destroy thee, that there shall be no inhabitant. And the sea coast shall be dwellings and cottages for shepherds, and folds for flocks." *Zephaniah 2:4-6*

Notice Gaza would be forsaken in verse 4. Gaza has been taken over many times but never just given away until Israel, under Ariel Sharon, handed it over to the Palestinians in AD 2005.

Zephaniah 2:7-8 describes the return of the modern nation of Israel. While Moab and Ammon (modern-day Jordan) will attack and occupy what will become known as the West Bank, the nation of Israel will control the sea coast including Ashdod, Ashkelon, and Gaza.

"And the coast shall be for the remnant of the house of Judah; they shall feed thereupon: in the houses of Ashkelon shall they lie down in the evening: for the LORD their God shall visit them, and turn away their captivity. I have heard the reproach of Moab, and the revilings of the children of Ammon, whereby they have reproached my people, and magnified themselves against their border." *Zephaniah 2:7-8*

Zephaniah 2:1-3 predicts that "the gathering" occurs sometime after Alexander the Great, and after the nation of Israel is established, and after the giving away of Gaza. Sometime after AD 2005 the "meek" will be hidden just before the Day of the Lord's anger comes. In other words, the Rapture of believers will occur before the seven-year period.

"Gather yourselves together, yea, gather together, O nation not desired; Before the decree bring forth, before the day pass as the chaff, before the fierce anger of the LORD come upon you, before the day of the LORD's anger come upon you. Seek ye the LORD, all ye meek of the earth, which have wrought his judgment; seek righteousness, seek meekness: it may be ye shall be hid in the day of the LORD's anger." *Zephaniah 2:1-3*

The Rapture occurs when Michael stands up.

The Rapture in Ancient Manuscripts

In the last few years I have been translating and publishing ancient manuscripts from the Dead Sea Scrolls and other places. Three of these have definite references to the pretribulational Rapture of the church, which is truly amazing in itself. The three are *The Book of Enoch, The Book of Gad the Seer* and *The Ezra Apocalypse.* Let's look closely at what these ancient works have to say.

Pretribulation Rapture from The Book of Enoch

The *Book of Enoch* was preserved by the Ethiopian Coptic church in their cannon of Scripture. It was rediscovered in the Dead Sea Scrolls.

As we noticed in the chapter on the pretribulational first century church, the apostle Paul used the term "out of the midst" in 2 Thessalonians 2:7 to refer to what is holding back the Day of the Lord. Church father Victor wrote a commentary on the book of Revelation. In 15.1 of his commentary, he uses the idiom "out of the midst" to refer to the Rapture of the church. What is interesting about this is that the *Book of Enoch* uses this same phrase in talking about Enoch himself as he is raptured from earth into heaven.

"And he was caught up on the chariots of the Spirit and his name taken *out of their midst.*"
Ancient Book of Enoch 70:2

In chapter 50 of the *Book of Enoch* he refers to the time when believers are changed into a glorious form. We know that is our resurrected bodies and that event occurs at the Rapture / Resurrection. See 1 Thessalonians 4:13-18 and

86

Daniel 12:2-3. He also says this event occurs at the time of the "Day of Tribulation." Notice that he also says the main reason for this event is to produce repentance in the hearts of the unbelievers.

"In those days *a change* will take place for the holy and elect, and the light of days will abide upon them, and glory and honour will turn to the holy. On the day of tribulation on which evil will gather against the sinners, the righteous will overcome in the name of the Lord of Spirits. He will cause the *others to witness it that they may repent* and cease the works of their hands." *Ancient Book of Enoch 50:1-2*

When many people who have been told about Christ, the Antichrist, and the Rapture and refuse to believe but then see the Rapture take place, it will cause many of them to repent. Of course, this will only work if they see the pre-trib Rapture and are left in the seven-year tribulation to have time to repent.

The Pretribulation Rapture from the Ezra Apocalypse
In the creation of the KJV 1611 Bible, the Catholics wanted the apocrypha included and the Protestants did not. A compromise was agreed on to include the Roman Catholic apocrypha in the middle of the Bible, so people would know it was not a part of either canon. Part of the compromise was that the middle section not only include the Roman Catholic apocrypha, but also one more book, *2 Esdras*. This book was included by the Anglicans because it accurately predicted the details of the partial fall of Rome and predicted the doom of Roman Catholicism. Unbeknownst to them it also predicted the rise of the "Dragon nations." These are the end time

The Rapture

Muslim armies. I have made a modern English translation of it entitled the *Ancient Apocalypse of Ezra*. It describes many things about the end times, but let's look at what it says about the Rapture.

The text says that those people who have survived the tribulation will see the return of the men who have never tasted death, but were caught up before the time of trouble began. The two witnesses of Revelation had not previously died, but will be killed by the Antichrist. So, at the beginning of the millennial reign, the only group of men who had never died but were now returning to earth could only be those who were in a pre-tribulational Rapture.

> "Everyone who survives all these things of which I have told you, will escape and see My deliverance and the end of the world. Then the men who have been taken up, who have not tasted death since their birth, will see it. Then the heart of the inhabitants of the earth will be transformed and changed into a different mind, for evil will be blotted out and deceit extinguished." *Ancient Apocalypse of Ezra 6:25-27*

In another place he calls that special group who have been taken from the earth will be brought back, "the bride." Their return will occur at the start of the millennial reign.

> "For behold the days to come, when the signs that I have foretold come to pass, the bride will be revealed, and what has now been withdrawn from the earth will be brought back. Whoever is delivered from these predicted evils, will see My wonders. For My Son,

the Messiah, will be revealed together with those who remain, and will rejoice with those who remain one thousand years." *Ancient Apocalypse of Ezra 7:26-28*

In 7:30, 43-44 we see a seven-day silence (seven-year tribulation period) which is a judgment that occurs before the Kingdom Age. In 12:34 we are told the remnant of believers are made joyful until the judgment is over, then they return. It is also interesting to note that in 2:33-41, those believers escape death by being "sealed" on a feast day.

The Pretribulation Rapture from Gad the Seer
Gad was a prophet in the time of King David. We are told in 1 Chronicles 29:29 that he wrote a book of prophecy. We finally obtained the Hebrew manuscript and published an English translation of it in 2016. It has many interesting topics; but in Chapter 14 we have a glimpse of a pre-tribulational rapture. The vision starts by a proclamation that it is judgment day, and an angel brings three sets of books before God who is seated on His throne. Judgment day is usually thought of as the Jewish new year, Rosh Hashanah, also called the Feast of Trumpets, and the Feast of the Awakening Blast. It is supposed to be the date of the Creation and the day of the Resurrection. The apostle Paul tells us that the Rapture happens within the twinkling of an eye at the same time as the Resurrection (see 1 Thessalonians 4:13-18).

The Book of Life is opened and those named in it receive eternal life that day. The books of the sinners are opened, and God says from His throne that He will wait until one-third through the month to give them another chance at repentance. One-third through the month, if this day was

89

The Rapture

Tishrei 1 (Rosh Hashanah), is Tishrei 10, or Yom Kippur, the Day of Atonement. The ritual performed on this day teaches about the destruction of the anti-Messiah and the establishment of the Kingdom Age. Rosh Hashanah is a two-day festival, and the seven days in between Rosh Hashanah and Yom Kippur are known as the Yamin Noraim, the terrible days. It is a picture of the seven-year tribulation period.

In this picture we have believers who are sinners, but forgiven, receiving eternal life. Those who missed the Rapture must wait until the end of the tribulation period to see Messiah. They must repent before that time or their names are moved into the third book and they will be damned for all eternity.

"And then a man dressed in linen brought before the glory of the LORD three books that contained the records of every man. And he read the first book and it contained the just deeds of His people, and the LORD said, "These are granted eternal life." And Satan said, "Who are these guilty people?" And the man dressed in linen cried to Satan like a <u>ram's horn</u> saying, "Silence! This day is holy to our Lord." And he read the second book, and it contained the unintentional sins of His people, and the LORD said, "Put that book aside, but save it, until <u>one third of the month passes by</u>, to see what they will do." And he read the third book, and it contained the wicked deeds of His people. And the LORD said to Satan, "These are your share. Take them and do what you want with them." And Satan took the wicked to a <u>waste land</u> to

90

destroy them there. And the man dressed in linen cried like a <u>ram's horn</u>, saying: "Blessed are the people who know the joyful shout [who look toward the Rapture], O LORD, who walk in the light of Your countenance." *The Ancient Book of Gad the Seer 14:7-14*

General Arguments Against Pretribulationalism

Some people believe the Rapture occurs at the end of the seven-year tribulation or at the Second Coming. These people are called posttribulationists. Those who believe the Rapture will occur somewhere in the middle of the seven-year period are called midtribulationists. We want to analyze several questions that people with those two viewpoints will often ask.

Why would we be better than all these other people that have suffered throughout history?
The persecutions of man are not necessarily the same thing as the wrath of God. God will not pour out His wrath on His children that are following Him to the best of their ability. Compare this with all the Scriptures stating we are not subject to His wrath.

The non-pretribulationists tend to not understand the difference between general tribulation throughout the centuries and the specific seven-year period called the tribulation.

Don't all the references to God saving us from the "wrath" simply mean that He is saving us from eternal hell?
No. At least two passages clearly refer to our being saved from the time of wrath/indignation by the Rapture and Resurrection.

In 1 Thessalonians 5, Paul is still on the topic of the "Day of the Lord" when he references the Rapture he spoke of in chapter 4. He states that God did not appoint us to *the* "wrath," but to obtain salvation when the dead and living are changed and live together with Him.

"For yourselves know perfectly that the day of the Lord so cometh as a thief in the night... For God hath not appointed us to wrath, but to obtain salvation by our Lord Jesus Christ, Who died for us, that, whether we wake or sleep, we should live together with him." *1 Thessalonians 5:2,9-10*

The prophet Isaiah states he knows he will resurrect with the other believers and they will all go into the "chedar" (wedding chambers) until the "indignation" is over. The "wrath" and "indignation" are terms for the "Day of the Lord."

"Thy dead men shall live, together with my dead body shall they arise. Awake and sing, ye that dwell in dust: for thy dew is as the dew of herbs, and the earth shall cast out the dead. Come, my people, enter thou into thy chambers, and shut thy doors about thee: hide thyself as it were for a little moment, until the indignation be overpast." *Isaiah 26:19-20*

The phrase "hide yourself for a little moment" can't mean hide in death until the Resurrection because thousands of years does not equal a "little moment." Nowhere in Scripture does the term "indignation" refer to those asleep in Jesus.

Note: the Greek word for wrath in New Testament Greek is indignation. The word translated indignation in Isaiah 26:20, (given above) is also used in the phrase "day of indignation" found in Ezekiel 22:24. So the words for wrath and indignation are used interchangeably. The "Day of Wrath" and "Day of Indignation" may not always refer to the Tribulation period, but they always refer to the time when God pours out His wrath on His enemies, but not on His children.

93

The Rapture

Is there any Scripture that states Jesus comes back before the seven-year period, the revealing of the Antichrist, or the Great Tribulation?

Not all three in one passage, no. But there are Scriptures that show Jesus coming back before the Rapture (1 Thessalonians 4); that the Rapture occurs before the Day of the Lord (1 Thessalonians 5); and that the Day of the Lord is the seven-year period (Amos 5); that the Great Tribulation is in that seven-year period (Matthew 24 and Daniel 11); and that the Antichrist is revealed at the beginning of the seven-year period (2 Thessalonians 2).

Couldn't the church be saved from the tribulation by being protected through it instead of Raptured before it comes?

No. The Minor Prophets and Revelation teach the saints (believers in the Messiah) will be killed in the greatest persecution of all time. So, the believers living during the Tribulation are not protected through the seven-year period.

What Scriptural proof do you offer that a prophecy about the coming of Jesus could be separated by seven years?

There are many examples in Scripture. In Luke 4 Jesus quotes Isaiah 61:1-2 but stops in the middle of a sentence. The last phrase of the sentence spoke of the judgment at His Second Coming. So, if one sentence of a prophecy can span 2,000 years of history, why can't one sentence about Jesus' Second Coming span only seven years?

The Jews teach the Abomination of Desolation was fulfilled by Antiochus Epiphanes in 165 BC.

In Matthew 24, Jesus said it was yet future in His time, about 32 AD.

Couldn't the Abomination of Desolation have taken place in 70 AD when the temple was destroyed?

No. Jesus said it occurs at the worse persecution ever, the Great Tribulation. The holocaust was worse than the time of the destruction of the temple; over six million Jews were slaughtered. So, the Great Tribulation must be yet future.

Jesus said only the Father knows the day and the hour of His Coming/Rapture. Since the Father does know, then the date is set in stone and can't be changed, so isn't the doctrine of immanency a false doctrine?

No. The doctrine of immanency just says *we* will not know when the Rapture will happen until it occurs. It is true that the Father has fixed the date; but it is still unknown to us.

Scriptural Objections Against Pretribulationism

In this chapter we want to examine the Scriptures that midtribulationists and posttribulationists use to argue against the pretribulationist position.

Daniel 7

Daniel 7:25 says the Antichrist will overcome the "saints." Doesn't that disprove a pretribulational Rapture?

No. The word "saint" can refer to any believer in Christ. The term "saint" includes church age believers, Old Testament believers, and Messianic believers who are saved after the pretribulational Rapture. Daniel 8:24 is clearly using the word to refer to the "holy people" and other nations. So, in these prophecies, the "saints" refers to the people in the nation of Israel and Gentiles that have become believers.

Daniel 9

Couldn't the gap between the 69th and 70th weeks in the prophecy given in Daniel 9 be something other than just the church age?

No. According to Acts 15, James stated it was the church age. See the chapter on the seven-year period for full details.

How do we know the Antichrist confirms the covenant in Daniel 9:27 instead of God or someone else?

It fits with 2 Thessalonians too well, and the disciples of the apostles all taught that this passage referred to the Antichrist. See the chapters on the pre-millennial first century church and pretribulational Rapture.

Daniel 12

Doesn't Michael standing up in Daniel 12 connect with Michael warring with the dragon in Revelation 12; which would lead to a midtribulational Rapture?

No. Michael stands up "at that time." If you refer back to the pervious chapter, the prophet is writing about the "time of the end" in which the Antichrist is attacked by Egypt, the king of the south. This happens in the first half of the seven-year period. So, when Michael stands up and the rescue, or Rapture, occurs with the Resurrection, it is at the *beginning* of the seven-year period.

Joel 2

Doesn't Joel 2:31 state the sun going dark is *before* the Day of the Lord?

We know the Day of the Lord is defined as the entire seven-year period by Amos 5:18, which says the Day of the Lord is when the animals attack. Revelation 6 shows the animals attacking in the first half of the seven-year period.

The two places where the "great and terrible" Day of the Lord occurs is here and in Malachi 4 where Elijah comes back. We know Elijah's 1260 days end at the sixth trump, so he comes before the middle of the seven years but not before the seven-year period starts. Therefore, we must conclude that the Day of the Lord is the seven-year period and "the great and terrible" part of it, is the wrath of the Lamb.

If a pretribulational Rapture does not occur, it will cause some to lose faith.

Not when they see nine out of ten prophecies about the revealing of the Antichrist take place. They will just wonder why they got one of the ten out of order and go back to search the Scriptures. See the chapter on the revealing of the Antichrist for full details.

Matthew 13
Doesn't the parable of the tares in Matthew 13 show a posttribulational Rapture?
No. This parable is referring to the judgment of the nations at the Second Coming. The parable in Matthew 25 calls this the judgment of the sheep and goats.

Matthew 24
Doesn't Jesus' statement "when you see the abomination," in Matthew 24:15, prove He is speaking to Christians and therefore the Rapture has not yet occurred?
No. There will be believers converted by the 144,000 during the seven-year tribulation, so there will always be believers present. If you have become a believer and are here to see the "abomination" in the temple in Jerusalem, Jesus warns you to flee! The ones who don't heed Jesus' warning could be the ones who are martyred by the Antichrist during the tribulation.

Doesn't the term "elect" in Matthew 24 refer to Christians, proving the Rapture did not occur at the beginning of the seven-year tribulation?
No. The term "elect" refers to believers. It has been applied to both Christians and Jewish believers in the Messiah alike. After the pretribulational Rapture of the church, there will be both Jewish and non-Jewish converts.

Couldn't the birth pangs be the first three and a half years of the seven-year period instead of the time before the seven-year period?
No. In Matthew 24, Jesus said the birth pangs occur prior to the time of the end. Daniel 11 defines the time of the end as the seven-year period when he specifically states the time of the end includes the Antichrist's war with Egypt. The birth pangs are prior to the start of the seven-year period.

Couldn't Jesus' warning about fleeing when they see the Abomination have been referring to Titus besieging the city in 70 AD?
If that were true, the seventy weeks would be over, and Jesus would be ruling from Jerusalem as anointed king!

Couldn't the destruction of the Jews in 70 AD be the Great Tribulation?
No. Jesus said the Great Tribulation will be worse than any other time before it. The Nazi holocaust was worse than the slaughter in AD 70; and if you take the prophecies literally, the Great Tribulation will be even worse than the holocaust was.

Matthew 24:26-27, 30-31 clearly teach that Jesus will not come back secretly, but for all to see. Doesn't this prove there is no secret Rapture?
No. These verses are talking about the Second Coming when Jesus returns to earth to set up the millennial kingdom. Verse 31 clearly teaches this occurs at the Great Trump.

Mark 13
Mark 13:27 presents the gathering at the Second Coming as coming *from* earth *to* heaven. Doesn't that prove a posttribulational Rapture?
No. Matthew clearly says His angels "will gather together His elect from the four winds, from one end of heaven to the other." This must mean from heaven to earth. Mark's phrase "from the four winds, from the uttermost part of the earth to the uttermost part of heaven" has to mean from the uttermost parts of the earth *and* heaven *to* Jerusalem. Remember, at this time the ones beheaded for Christ's sake are resurrected (Rev. 20:4-5), so the raptured saints are returning to earth, and the tribulation saints are being resurrected.

The Rapture
Luke 17
Luke 17:37, as well as Matthew 24:28, depicts some people being taken, while others are left. Jesus says they are taken to where the vultures gather to eat the corpse. How could this be the Rapture?
There are four groups of people who are taken somewhere.

1. Those Raptured from earth to heaven by God.
   1 Thessalonians 4:11-18
2. Those driven by demons to Armageddon.
   Revelation 16:13-16
3. Those taken by force from Jerusalem by the Antichrist and put to death.
   Matthew 24:15-22; Zechariah 14:2
4. Those taken by God into the fire at the sheep/goat judgment.
   Matthew 25:31-46

Of these four, the only ones going to where the birds eat their flesh are those driven by demons to Armageddon. God does not take them anywhere.

Understand the disciples spoke in Hebrew or Aramaic and their direct quotes were written into Greek and translated into English. We must look for Hebrew idioms. "Where?" in Hebrew can mean "where to" or "where from" not just "where" like in English.

This being the case, the only group that is being taken away from where God's Wrath is poured out and the Battle of Armageddon occurs, are the raptured believers. They are being taken from earth to heaven to avoid the wrath.

Acts 3

Doesn't Acts 3:21 state Jesus must remain in heaven until the tribulation is over, thus proving a posttribulational Rapture?

No. Jesus remains in heaven until the "period of restoration of all things."

> "whom heaven must receive until the period of restoration of all things about which God spoke by the mouth of His holy prophets from ancient time."
> *Acts 3:21 NASV*

Peter clearly says in this passage the "period of restoration of all things" was a favorite topic of the prophets. In Matthew 17:11 Jesus says Elijah must come and "restore all things." This is in reference to Elijah coming before the great and terrible Day of the Lord in Malachi 4:5-6.

> "And Jesus answered and said unto them, Elias truly shall first come, and restore all things." *Matthew 17:11*

The period of restoring all things includes Elijah preaching 1260 days during the seven-year period. The period of restoration is the seven-year period. So, Jesus remains in heaven until the Rapture, which occurs at the start of the seven-year period.

1 Corinthians 15

Doesn't the "Last Trump" of 1 Corinthians 15 refer to the seventh trumpet in Revelation 11?

No. The apostle Paul died in the year AD 67. The apostle John wrote the book of Revelation in AD 95, during the reign of Emperor Domitian. The Book of Revelation was written almost thirty years *after* Paul died, so Paul was not referring to the seventh trump.

The Rapture

The seven festivals ordained by God teach prophecy by their rituals. Each of the seven festivals have multiple names that help describe what that festival's ritual teaches. The festival of Pentecost is called the festival of the First Trump. The festival of Rosh Hashanah is named the festival of the "Last Trump." The festival of the "Day of Atonement" (or Yom Kippur in Hebrew) is called the festival of the Great Trump. One can verify these by looking up these terms in the Encyclopedia Judaica.

See Appendix B for complete details.

1 Thessalonians 4

How do we know that the catching up in 1 Thessalonians 4 has not already occurred?

It was yet future in Paul's time. Paul was beheaded in June of 67 AD. The catching up is at the time of the return of Jesus Christ, which is within seven years of the establishment of the millennial reign. This false teaching was the reason why Paul felt prompted by the Holy Spirit to write 2 Thessalonians.

1 Thessalonians 5

In 1 Thessalonians 5 Paul writes "that day" will not overtake Christians like a thief. Doesn't that mean that Christians will know when the Rapture will occur because it is at the middle or end of the Tribulation period?

No. The sudden *destruction* of "that day," the Day of the Lord or seven-year period, will not overtake Christians. Christians leaving earth in a pretribulational Rapture will leave non-Christians to be surprised by this destruction.

2 Thessalonians 1

Doesn't 2 Thessalonians 1:7 show the church's suffering will be relieved (raptured) when Jesus comes with His angels at the Second Coming?

No. This passage is saying the church's suffering will be relieved (raptured), *then* the period of God's fiery wrath will be poured out by the angels (trumpet and bowl judgments). The relief comes *before* the seven-year period.

2 Thessalonians 2

Doesn't 2 Thessalonians state the Antichrist will be revealed when he sits in the Temple?

No. The revealing is when he confirms the covenant at the start of the seven-year period. The confirming of the covenant sparks nine other prophecies that clearly reveal the Antichrist at the start of the seven-year period. See the chapter on the revealing of the Antichrist for details.

If the Holy Spirit was the restrainer, couldn't He be removed and leave the church to be Raptured at a later time?

No. The Scripture says, "he will never leave us or forsake us." The Holy Spirit will not leave the earth and leave believers here on their own – that would break God's promise and make Him a liar.

Couldn't the Restrainer of 2 Thessalonians 2 be something other than the Holy Spirit and the church, thus leaving the Rapture for another time?

No. Nothing other than the Holy Spirit fits scripturally with Paul's teaching in 2 Thessalonians 2. Isaiah 33 seems to indicate this also. See the chapter on the pretribulational Rapture for a full discussion on this topic.

The Rapture
How do we know the gathering mentioned in 2 Thessalonians 2 is the Rapture and not the one at the Second Coming?
Because we are taken to the Lord and not from the ends of the earth and heaven to Jerusalem.

Revelation 6
Couldn't the verses that say we will be saved from "the Wrath" mean the "Lamb's wrath" which is in the last three and a half years, and therefore teach a midtribulational Rapture?
No. The Lamb's wrath is the trumpet and bowl judgments that do occur in the last three and a half years of the seven-year period, but the Day of Wrath, or the Day of the Lord as we have seen, is the whole seven-year period.

2 Peter 3
Doesn't 2 Peter 3:3-4 teach that people will not believe in the coming of Jesus because a pretribulational Rapture was taught, and when it did not happen, they rejected the whole of end time prophecy from the Bible?
No. Peter here is saying they will be willingly ignorant of the historicity of Genesis and the prophecies of the end times. This prophecy has already come to pass in many churches. They reject Genesis as history by accepting evolution instead of creationism. They also reject the end time prophecies (like the Rapture and seven-year period) in favor of uniformitarianism.

Revelation 20
Doesn't Revelation 20:4-6 teach the resurrection of believers, and therefore the Rapture, occur at the Second Coming?
Looking at this passage closely, it states those who were martyred during the tribulation will be resurrected at the Second Coming. The term "first resurrection" means the first

Scriptural Objections
type of resurrection, that of the believers who inherit eternal life. It is contrasted with the Second Death, which is the resurrection to eternal damnation which occurs at the Great White Throne judgment.

We have to interpret "first resurrection" as the first *type* of resurrection because there have already been several resurrections of the first type. Matthew 27:52-53 records that many saints resurrected and ascended with Jesus.

Questions for Non-pretribulationalists

Q 1

If the Rapture / Resurrection occurs at the end of the seven-year period and at that time believers are given glorified bodies which "neither give or are given in marriage," then who populates the earth during the Millennium?

The two witnesses are also resurrected with glorified bodies and the 144,000 are men who have never known a woman.

Q 2

True believers knew the day and hour of the first coming after the decree came to rebuild Jerusalem. True believers will know when the Second Coming will take place when the seven-year period begins. Jesus said no one will know the day or hour of the Rapture of the church. Doesn't this prove that the Rapture could not be in the middle or end of the seven-year period? Otherwise believers will know the exact day and hour of the Rapture. So, there must be a pretribulational Rapture.

Q 3

If the Antichrist overcomes the saints during the seven-year period, and Jesus said the gates of hell will not prevail against the church (Matthew 16:18), doesn't that prove a pretribulational Rapture?

Appendix A
Definitions

Abomination of Desolation
The abomination occurs when the Antichrist places an idol or a teraphim in the new Jerusalem temple, then sits in the Temple himself professing to be God incarnate.

The Antichrist
The Antichrist is the evil one who persecutes believers during the seven-year period. He is also called the son of perdition, the man of sin.

The Apostasy
The apostasy is the turning away from biblical doctrine to demonic doctrine in the last days. The apostasy can't completely be fulfilled until the true church is raptured away. See the chapter on the apostasy for full details.

Asleep in Christ
Those "asleep in Christ" are believers who have died believing in Jesus as their savior. This is defined in 1 Thessalonians 4:13-17.

Birth Pangs
Jesus uses the term birth pangs to refer to the time before the seven-year period. Ideally it is from the 1948 return of the nation of Israel to the Rapture of the church. See the chapter on the birth pangs for full details.

The "Catching Up"
This is the term the apostle Paul gives for the Rapture in 1 Thessalonians 4.

The Rapture

Church Age
The church age is the time between the 69th and 70th weeks of Daniel's seventy-week prophecy. It contains the dates 32, 130, 132, and 1948 AD.

Coming in the Clouds
This is a phrase used in Daniel 7:13 for what the New Testament calls the Second Coming, the time when the Antichrist, or beast, is destroyed.

The Covenant
This is a peace covenant created for Israelis and Palestinians, but never enforced until the Antichrist enforces it.

Daniel's Seventieth Week
The last seven years before the return of Jesus and the set up of His millennial kingdom. See Daniel 9:27.

Day of Christ
The Day of Christ is the title Paul uses for the seven-year period in 2 Thessalonians 2. See the chapter on the pretribulational Rapture for full details.

Day of the Lord
The Day of the Lord is the seven-year tribulation period. This is different than the Great and Terrible Day of the Lord. See the chapter on the Day of the Lord for details.

Day of Wrath
This is another name for the Day of the Lord or the seven-year period usually called the tribulation.

Days Cut Short
Jesus "cuts short" the time of the Antichrist's persecution of Jews by sending the trumpet plagues. If Jesus did not cut the days short, the Antichrist would kill every last one of the saints. See the chapter on what Jesus said for details.

The Delusion

The delusion is the false belief that the Antichrist is the true Messiah. This will cause people who have chosen not to study the Scriptures to take the mark of the beast. This will also cause them to go to hell when they die.

End Time, Time of the End, End of the Age/World

These are all terms for the seven-year tribulation. See Daniel 8:17,19; 11:35,40; 12:4,9; Matthew 24:3,6,13,14; 28:20. Hebrews 9:26 uses the term "end of the world" to describe the end of the Jewish age.

The Elect

The elect are the believers in Christ. In this age it is the church. After the Rapture, it will be mainly messianic believers, then eventually all believing Israel.

Falling Away

The falling away is the phrase Paul uses in 2 Thessalonians 2 to refer to the apostasy. See the chapter on the pretribulational Rapture for full details.

First Resurrection

The first resurrection is the first *kind* of resurrection, that of believers unto eternal life. It is the opposite of the Second Death, which is the resurrection of the damned at the Great White Throne judgment. This is explained in Revelation 20:4.

First Trump

The festival of the First Trump is another name for the festival of Pentecost. See Appendix B, the Rabbinic Festivals, for full details.

The Gathering

The gathering is a term that refers to our Lord Jesus gathering His people to a certain place. In 1 Thessalonians 4

The Rapture

we are told the Rapture gathers us to Him in the clouds. In Matthew 24 we are told that at the Second Coming the raptured believers are gathered back from the ends of the heavens and the believers that made it through the seven-year period are gathered from the four corners of the earth.

Great and Terrible Day of the Lord
This is a title for the Wrath of the Lamb, which is poured out during the last half of the seven-year period, called the Day of the Lord. See the chapter on the Day of the Lord for details.

Great Tribulation
The Antichrist's persecution of the Jews during the last half of the seven-year period.

Great Trump
This is the Second Coming when raptured saints are gathered from heaven back to earth. The festival of the Great Trump is another name of the festival of the Day of Atonement. See Appendix B, the Rabbinic Festivals, for full details.

Great White Throne Judgment
This is the judgment of all the unsaved occurring at the end of the millennial reign of Jesus Christ. It is also called the Second Death to contrast it with the first resurrection.

The Indignation
The term indignation can refer to any wrath in the past, present, or future. The Day of Indignation refers to the Day of the Lord or the seven-year period. See the chapter on the Day of the Lord for details.

Last Trump
The Last Trump is one of the names given to the festival of Rosh Hashanah, or Trumpets. Midtribulationists often mistake Paul's reference to the Last Trump in 1 Corinthians 15:52 for the seventh and last trumpet judgment in the book

of Revelation. See Appendix B, the Rabbinic Festivals for full details.

Love of the Truth
A real Christian understands that the Bible is the literal word of God. When they study it closely and believe the prophecies are literal and take them very seriously, they are said to have a "love of the truth." Those who profess to be Christians but don't care enough to take time to study the prophecies do not have a love for the truth but love the things of the world more than Christ. These will be deceived when the Antichrist works his lying signs and wonders, simply because they do not know any better because they did not study the Bible. They had "no love of the truth."

Manifestation of the Sons of God
The Rapture, when believers' physical bodies become glorified with immortality.

Michael Standing Up
The beginning of the seven-year period, referenced in Daniel 12.

Millennial Kingdom
This is the time when Jesus returns to earth and sets up a worldwide kingdom that literally lasts for 1,000 years. During this time Jesus Christ personally and physically reigns from the city of Jerusalem, Israel.

Mystery of Lawlessness
The mystery of lawlessness is the name for the apostasy that was occurring in Paul's time. It was started by the Gnostic cults. It is the forerunner of the end time apostasy.

The Rapture
The future event where both the dead in Christ resurrect and the living in Christ are changed into an immortal form. Both are then taken as one group to meet the Lord in the air.

Redemption of our Bodies
The Rapture, when believers' physical bodies become glorified with immortality.

Reincarnation
Reincarnation is the false belief that spirits of the dead return to earth in a different body. This is the opposite of resurrection.

The Restrainer
The restrainer is the Holy Spirit. He restrains the revealing of the Antichrist.

Resurrection
A resurrection is when the dead are brought back to life in their physical form. This is the opposite of the false belief of reincarnation.

The Retribution
The retribution is a term used for God's wrath being poured out during the tribulation period.

Revealing of the Antichrist
This is the beginning of the seven-year period. The Antichrist reveals himself by fulfilling ten prophecies. See the chapter on the revealing of the Antichrist.

Second Death
The second death is the resurrection of all the damned at the Great White Throne Judgment at the end of the millennial reign of Jesus Christ. Those whose names are not written in the book of life are cast into the lake of fire.

Seventieth Week
The last seven years before the return of Jesus when He sets up His millennial kingdom. See Daniel 9:27.

Seventh Trump
The last of the seven trumpet judgments recorded in Revelation 15. This is often confused with the "last trump" that Paul described as the time of the Resurrection and Rapture. The apostle Paul was actually referring to the festival of the "Last Trump" which is another name for the festival of Rosh Hashanah. See Appendix B, the Rabbinic Festivals, for full details.

Sign of the Son of Man
The return of Christ to earth.

Sun Darkened
The prophet Joel in Joel 2 and Jesus in Matthew 24 both refer to the sun going dark and the moon not giving light as marking the beginning of the Wrath of the Lamb, which occurs in the last half of the seven-year tribulation. It is in response to the Antichrist's major persecution of Jews and believers.

The Temple
The temple is the Jewish temple of God that will sit on top of Mount Moriah in Jerusalem, Israel. The last one was destroyed by the Roman general Titus, in AD 70. As of AD 2018, the next temple has yet to be built. Prophecy dictates it will be rebuilt soon.

Thief in the Night
This term is used to denote the suddenness and unexpectedness of the destruction that starts at the beginning of the Day of the Lord. It shows no one will know when the Rapture will happen, since that event will start the Day of the Lord. First Thessalonians 5 indicates the sudden destruction

The Rapture
will not catch believers as a thief in the night because we are not appointed to wrath.

Time of Distress

The time of distress is the term used in Daniel 12 for the seven-year period.

The Tribulation

The word tribulation generally means persecution. In Matthew 24 Jesus used the word to refer to the greatest persecution ever, the Antichrist's persecution of believers, starting at the middle of the seven-year period. Today, among fundamentalist Christians, the term "tribulation" most often refers to the entire seven-year period before the establishment of the millennial kingdom.

The Wrath

This can refer to any period when God pours out His judgment in the past, present, or the future. In 1 Thessalonians 5, Paul clearly uses the term to refer to the Day of the Lord.

The Wrath of the Lamb

This term refers to the wrath of the trumpet and bowl judgments as described in the book of Revelation. This period is also called the Great and Terrible Day of the Lord.

Appendix B
The Rabbinic Festivals

God ordained seven festivals for the Jews to observe, as recorded in Leviticus 23. Four occur in the spring and three occur in the fall.

The spring festivals, in order, are: Passover, Unleavened Bread, First Fruits, and Pentecost. The rituals performed on these spring festivals prophetically teach about the first coming of the Messiah. The fall festivals, in order, are: Trumpets, Atonement, and Tabernacles. The rituals performed on these fall festivals prophetically teach about the Second Coming of the Messiah.

To see the prophetical patterns, we will look at Passover first, because it is so well documented. After Passover we will look at parts of the rituals of Trumpets and Atonement as they pertain to our Rapture study.

Passover
Passover occurs on the fourteenth day of Nissan. From its very beginning it commemorated the Exodus from Egypt. The festival of Unleavened Bread occurs on the fifteenth of Nissan and continues for one week. First Fruits is the weekly sabbath after Unleavened Bread. This varies from year to year, but on the year the Messiah was crucified, it occurred on the seventeenth of Nissan.

The people observed the Passover in the home with a ritual called the Seder.

Passover Seder
The Seder starts at 6 pm and must be finished by midnight. A special cloth container with three stacked pockets called a Matzah-Tash sits on the table containing a loaf of

115

unleavened bread in each pocket (symbolizing the Trinity). The middle loaf of unleavened bread, or Matzah, is taken out and torn in two. The smaller piece is placed back in the middle pocket between the other two. The larger piece is wrapped in a napkin and hidden, (symbolizing the death and burial of the second person of the Trinity, the Son). It will be used later for the Afikomen. Then the story of the Exodus from Egypt is told, and the group sings Psalms 113-114.

Note that the Matzah is pierced and has stripes from being cooked unleavened. Compare this to Isaiah 53.

After that, the father brings out the lower piece of Matzah from the Matzah-Tash, blesses it, then each member eats a small piece of the bread. This symbolized the Holy Spirit, third person of the Trinity. Next, the Passover meal is eaten, which may take an hour or two.

After the meal the father sends the children to hunt for hidden Matzah. The Seder cannot continue until the Matzah is found and given back to the father. This symbolizes the resurrection and ascension of the Messiah. The child negotiates what gift the father will give him for returning the Matzah, then the father gives the child a coin as a down payment for the gift, the matzah is returned, and the Seder continues. This gift of a coin referred to as "the promise of the father" symbolizes the giving of the Holy Spirit at Pentecost as an earnest deposit of the gift of eternal life.

Next the father brings out the Matzah that was hidden, and each member is given two pieces of matzah to make the Afikomen. The Afikomen is a sandwich made of two pieces of matzah with the Maror (bitter herbs) on one side and the Charoset (a sweet antidote to the bitter herbs) on the other side. The sandwich is eaten Maror side first, then the Charoset. This act symbolizes that the Messiah is the only antidote for sin.

116

Since it was forbidden to eat the Passover lamb anywhere except Jerusalem (Deuteronomy 16:5), together the group says, "I am observing this commandment, so I may remember the Passover lamb eaten at the end of the Seder. May the eating of the Afikomen achieve all the spiritual things accomplished by the Passover lamb itself."

During the last plague in Egypt before the Exodus, if one placed the blood of the Passover lamb on the door post of the home, the death angel would not kill the first born in the house. Salvation was given if you believed in the safety represented by the blood of the Passover lamb.

Finally, they sing Psalm 126 and drink the third cup of wine. Then the fourth cup, the cup of Elijah is poured, and they sing the Hallel - Psalms 115-118, and 136.

Passover in the Temple
In the time of Jesus, the high priest, on the 10th of Nisan, would go to Bethany to get an unblemished lamb and bring it into the Temple to be inspected for four days. As the lamb was brought to the eastern gate, pilgrims would line the sides, wave palm branches and say, "Baruch Ha Shem Adonai." This is Hebrew for "blessed be the name of the Lord," and is a quote from Psalm 118:26-27. Jesus left the house of Lazarus in Bethany on the tenth to teach in the temple. At the temple, the scribes asked their hardest questions of Jesus and walked away saying, "never a man spoke as this man." At 9 AM on the fourteenth of Nisan, the lamb was tied to one of the horns of the altar and at 3 PM the high priest would slay the lamb while saying the words "It is finished." These words were said when any "shelem" or peace offering was sacrificed.

Jesus was placed on the Cross at 9 AM and died at 3 PM. The apostle Paul taught this many times and wrote in 1 Corinthians:

The Rapture

> "Get rid of the old yeast so that you may be a new
> batch of dough, since you are to be free from yeast.
> For the Messiah, our Passover, has been sacrificed."
> *1 Corinthians 5:7 ISV*

Jesus was crucified on the fourteenth of Nisan and
resurrected three days later on the seventeenth of Nisan. The
ritual of firstfruits taught about the resurrection of the
Messiah. The apostle Paul even connected that festival with
Jesus' resurrection by saying:

> "But now is Christ risen from the dead, and become
> the firstfruits of them that slept." *1 Corinthians 15:20*

Pentecost - First Trump
The festival of Pentecost takes place fifty days after
Passover. The children of Israel left Egypt on the night of the
fifteenth of Nissan. They traveled through the Red Sea to
Mount Sinai. Moses gave instructions to the children of
Israel, then went up the mountain of God. Moses came down
the mountain forty days later on the sixth of Sivan, or
Pentecost.

Paul wrote in Hebrews 12:19 that the voice coming from
Mount Sinai sounded like a trumpet. The ancient rabbis
referred to the festival of Pentecost as the festival of the First
Trump. They connected the festival with the ram that was
sacrificed by Abraham in place of Isaac. They said the left
horn represented the birth of Israel and the right horn
represented Israel's complete restoration when the Messiah
comes.

Christians are aware that the festival of Pentecost also
represents the birth of the church.

About Pentecost, one Jewish legend says:

"When God gave the Law on Mt. Sinai, He displayed untold marvels to Israel with His voice. What happened? God spoke and the voice reverberated throughout the whole land... it says, the people witnessed the thunderings (Exodus 18:15). Note that it does not say "the thunder," but "the thunderings;" wherefore Rabbi Johanan said that God's voice, as it was uttered, split into 70 languages, so that all the nations should understand." *Exodus Rabbah 5:9*

In another legend not only does God's voice split into seventy languages, but can be seen visibly as tongues of fire coming upon the carved stones to produce the Ten Commandments. See *The Midrash Says on Shemot* by Rabbi Moshe Weissman, pg. 182 for full details on these and other legends.

"The Revelation at Sinai, it was taught, was given in desert territory, which belongs to one nation exclusively; and it was not heard by Israel alone, but by the inhabitants of all the earth. The Divine Voice divided itself into the seventy tongues then spoken on the earth, so that all the children of men might understand its world-embracing and man-redeeming message." Rabbi Joseph Hertz, Authorized Daily Prayer Book, pg. 791

What is interesting about these legends is that about 1,500 years later, on another Pentecost, as the Holy Spirit was given at the birth of the church, cloven tongues of fire could be seen resting on the heads of believers. Then the believers spoke in other tongues. Acts 2 lists seventeen different foreign languages, but I believe it was a lot more.

"And how hear we every man in our own tongue, wherein we were born? Parthians, and Medes, and Elamites, and the dwellers in Mesopotamia, and in

119

The Rapture

Judaea, and Cappadocia, in Pontus, and Asia, Phrygia, and Pamphylia, in Egypt, and in the parts of Libya about Cyrene, and strangers of Rome, Jews and proselytes, Cretes and Arabians, we do hear them speak in our tongues the wonderful works of God." *Acts 2:8-11*

Peter recorded that all these things were a partial fulfillment of the prophecy given by Joel:

"But this is that which was spoken by the prophet Joel; And it shall come to pass in the last days, saith God, I will pour out of My Spirit upon all flesh: and your sons and your daughters shall prophesy, and your young men shall see visions, and your old men shall dream dreams: And on My servants and on My handmaidens I will pour out in those days of My Spirit; and they shall prophesy: And I will shew wonders in heaven above, and signs in the earth beneath; blood, and fire, and vapour of smoke: The sun shall be turned into darkness, and the moon into blood, before the great and notable day of the Lord come: And it shall come to pass, that whosoever shall call on the name of the Lord shall be saved." *Acts 2:16-21*

Cloven tongues of fire and multiple foreign languages were said to have taken place both at the birth of Israel and the birth of the church. Each time these events occurred they were on a Pentecost, or festival of the First Trump.

Trumpets - Last Trump
The festival of Trumpets is also known by several names. Rosh Ha Shannah, meaning the head of the year, or New Year's Day, is one name. It is also called Yom ha-Din, Day of Judgment, and Yom ha-Zikkaron, the Day of Remembrance, by the ancient rabbis. Another name for this

festival is Yom Turah, meaning the day of the awakening blast. This name is taken from Leviticus 23:24.

"Speak unto the children of Israel, saying, In the seventh month, in the first day of the month, shall ye have a sabbath, a memorial of blowing of trumpets, an holy convocation." *Leviticus 23:24*

The one Hebrew word translated here as "blowing of trumpets" is the Hebrew word "turah." It is normally used to refer to a trumpet blast that awakens troops. The ancient rabbis taught this prophetically referred to the time of the Resurrection.

"The resurrection of the dead will occur on Yom haDin, which is also called Rosh haShannah," *Talmud, Rosh haShannah 16b*

"It has been taught: Rabbi Eliezer says, 'In the month of Tishri the world was created, ...and in Tishrei they will be redeemed in the time to come.'" *Talmud, Rosh haShannah 10b-11a*

Rabbi Herman Kieval wrote *The High Holy Days,* which was first published in 1959. In his work he states that many Jewish scholars, including Theodore Gaster, have taught that the festival of Rosh Hashanah was called the festival of the Last Trump from ancient times.

In an ancient Jewish midrash called *Prike deR' Eliezer* the origin of these terms is explained.

The left horn of the ram sacrificed by Abraham in place of Isaac, is called the First Trump, and was blown on Mount Sinai. Its right horn, called the Last Trump, will be blown to herald the coming of the Messiah.

The Rapture
Notice in 1 Corinthians, Paul uses festival language a number of times. In 1 Corinthians 5:6-7 Jesus is our Passover lamb, and in 1 Corinthians 5:8 we keep the feast with Unleavened Bread. All through chapters 11-14 Jesus is connected with the Feast of Weeks and in 1 Corinthians 15:20-23 Jesus is our Firstfruits. So, when Paul states the Rapture will occur at the last trump, it should be clear he is referring to the festival of the Last Trump, or Rosh Hashanah.

> "Behold, I shew you a mystery; We shall not all sleep, but we shall all be changed, In a moment, in the twinkling of an eye, at the last trump: for the trumpet shall sound, and the dead shall be raised incorruptible, and we shall be changed."
> *1 Corinthians 15:51-52*

Paul does not necessarily mean that the Rapture will occur on the very day of Rosh Hashanah, but that the ritual performed on Rosh Hashanah prophetically teaches on the Rapture!

Part of the ritual for Rosh Hashanah consists of the "Zikhronot," or Book of Remembrance being opened and the "Natzal" occurring. Natzal is the Hebrew word that corresponds to the Greek word "harpazo." Harpazo is the New Testament Greek word we translate as "rapture."

In discussing the Rapture in 1 Thessalonians 4 and 5, Paul states that of the "times and seasons" you should not be ignorant. This refers to the seven festivals that prophetically teach about the coming of our Lord.

Why the "Last Trump" is Not the Seventh Trump.
Many Christians who are ignorant of the seven festivals *assume* that the "last trump" Paul talked about in 1 Corinthians 15:52-53 is the same as the seventh trumpet

The Rabbinic Festivals
recorded in Revelation 11:15. One major problem with this point of view is that Paul wrote 1 Corinthians before his death in AD 67. John wrote the book of Revelation in AD 95. Paul could not be quoting a book written more than 25 years after his death! Knowing these things let us go on and see what we can learn about the seven-year tribulation period from these festivals.

Day of Concealment
Another term for Rosh Hashanah is Yom haKeseh. Yom haKeseh means "the Day of Concealment." The term was taken from Psalm 81:3 by the ancient rabbis.

"Blow up the trumpet in the new moon, in the time appointed, on our solemn feast day." *Psalm 81:3*

The Hebrew word "Keseh" is translated "new moon" in this passage. A new moon is said to be concealed as opposed to a full moon. This is yet another picture of the concealment of the church by the Rapture.

Days of Awe
The chart on the next page shows the outline of this time period with the fall festivals. The New Year starts with Rosh HaShannah (RHS). This is a two-day festival occurring on the first and second of Tishrei.

"From the time of R. Johanan b. Zakkai; Palestine, like other countries, observed Rosh ha-Shanah for two days. The Zohar lays stress on the universal observance of two days." *Jewishencyclopedia.com; New-Year*

Tishrei occurs during our September/October. This festival is also called Yom Teruah, which means the "day of the awakening blast." The Bible refers to the day as "The Day of the Blowing of the Shofar" (Yom Teruah, Leviticus 23:24),

123

The Rapture

and rabbinic literature and the liturgy itself describe Rosh Hashanah as "The Day of Judgment" (Yom ha-Din) and "The Day of Remembrance" (Yom ha-Zikkaron). Jewish tradition says this is the day when the Resurrection will occur. Paul tells us the Resurrection and the Rapture will occur on the same day in the twinkling of an eye.

The tenth of Tishrei is the festival of Yom Kippur (YK), which means the "Day of Atonement." The ritual performed on Yom Kippur teaches about the destruction of the Antichrist and the Second Coming of the Messiah.

The time between Rosh Hashanah and Yom Kippur are called the Yomin Noraim, which means the "days of awe" or the terrible days. The ancient rabbis took this name from Joel 2:11, which refers to the Day of the Lord.

> "The LORD utters His voice before His army; surely His camp is very great, for strong is he who carries out His word. The day of the LORD is indeed great and very awesome [Nora], and who can endure it?" *Joel 2:11*

Notice, the Yomin Noraim are the seven days/years that occur between the Rapture/Resurrection and the Second Coming! This gives a perfect picture of the pretribulational Rapture of the Church.

> "and to wait for His Son from heaven, whom He raised from the dead, that is Jesus, who **rescues** us from the wrath to come." *1 Thessalonians 1:10*

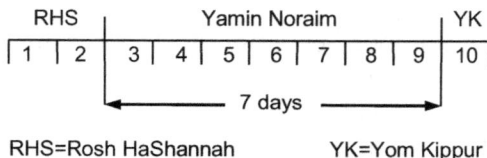

RHS=Rosh HaShannah   YK=Yom Kippur

124

Day of Atonement - Great Trump

The Festival of Trumpets is called the Festival of "The Awakening Blast" and the "Last Trump." In contrast with this, the festival of the Day of Atonement is called the Festival of the "Great Trump."

This helps us organize the prophecies in Scripture. Whenever we see "last trump" in Scripture, we know it is referring to the time of the Rapture/Resurrection of believers. Whenever we see the "great trump" we know it is referring to the Second Coming. To verify the different festival names, look them up in the Encyclopedia Judaica.

During the festival of Yom Kippur there is a prophetic ceremony that involves two goats. Two nearly identical goats are selected and brought before the high priest. The high priest places his

Newly created lots for
the Yom Kippur ceremony

hands on one of the goats. Another priest brings out the Qalephi, a box containing two lots.

One of the lots is randomly withdrawn by the high priest and placed with the first goat. Then the other is withdrawn for the second goat. On one lot is engraved לאדני, meaning "for the Lord." The goat that randomly acquired the lot "for the Lord" is sacrificed for the sins of the people. This animal is a perfect representation of the Messiah dying for the sins of the world. The other lot is engraved with לעזאזל, meaning "for Azazel." This has commonly been translated "scapegoat," but Azazel actually is a proper name. Moses wrote about this ceremony in Leviticus 16 saying:

> "Aaron shall cast lots for the two goats, one lot for the LORD and the other lot for the scapegoat

125

The Rapture
[Azazel]. Then Aaron shall offer the goat on which the lot for the LORD fell, and make it a sin offering. But the goat on which the lot for the scapegoat fell shall be presented alive before the LORD, to make atonement upon it, to send it into the wilderness as the scapegoat [to Azazel]." *Leviticus 16:8-10*

The Mishnah is a book written about AD 200. It contains the Oral Torah, or the exact details of how to perform the rituals mentioned the Old Testament. In Yoma 4.2 of the Mishnah, details are given concerning the ceremony of the two goats.

A scarlet-colored wool cord was specially created for this ceremony. One piece of this cord was tied to one of the horns of the Azazel goat. One piece of the cord was tied around the neck of the Lord's goat.

In Leviticus, it describes the Azazel goat being sent into the "wilderness." But the Mishnah gives greater detail about that part of the ritual in Yoma 6. The two goats must be alike in appearance, size, and weight. The "wilderness" that the Azazel goat was taken to was actually a ravine. Between Jerusalem and this ravine were ten stations or booths. Since it was a High Holy Day one could not travel very far. One priest took the Azazel goat from Jerusalem to the first booth. Then another priest took it from the second to the third booth. This continued until a priest took it from the tenth booth to the ravine. Anciently this ravine was called Bet HaDudo. Its whereabouts is currently unknown. The Mishnah then says the priest took the crimson cord off of the goat and tied one piece to the large rock on the cliff of the ravine, and he tied the other piece to the horns of the goat. He then pushed the goat off the cliff. Before it would be halfway down the cliff, it was already torn into pieces.

If the ritual was properly done, the crimson cord would turn snow white. At that point the priest would signal the tenth

126

booth, which would in turn signal the ninth, all the way back to the first booth, which would signal the high priest standing at the door of the sanctuary. When the high priest learned the crimson thread had turned white, he finished the ritual by quoting Isaiah 1:18

"'Come now, and let us reason together,' says the LORD, 'though your sins are as scarlet, they will be as white as snow; though they are red like crimson, they will be like wool.'" *Isaiah 1:18*

The Meaning of the Ritual
It has been speculated that the scapegoat represents Jesus taking away our sin. That is one possible interpretation. If the information given in the Mishnah is correct, another picture emerges. Two identical goats, one dedicated to God, the other dedicated to Satan. One goat represents the Messiah and the other represents the Antichrist. The ravine represents, and probably is located in, the valley of Megiddo. The only way to tell the difference between the Messiah and the Antichrist is to know the Lord's will by carefully studying the Word of God. At the Second Coming, the Antichrist will be destroyed in Megiddo, in a battle called Armageddon.

Appendix C
Recently Fulfilled Prophecies

The following is a chart from the book *Ancient Prophecies Revealed*. It lists fifty plus prophecies that have been fulfilled since Israel became a nation in AD 1948. These, plus the next fifteen yet-to-be fulfilled prophecies, are given for your information. For a detailed description of these and many others, see *Ancient Prophecies Revealed*.

Date	Prophecy	References
1948	1. Israel will be reestablished as a nation	Isa. 11:11
	2. British ships will be the first to bring the Jewish people home	Isa. 60:9
	3. Israel will come back as one nation, not two	Hosea 1:11; Ezek. 37:18 ,19,22
	4. The nation of Israel will be born in a day	Isa. 66:8
	5. Israel will be reestablished by a leader named David	Hosea 3:5
	6. The revived state will be named "Israel"	Ezek. 37:11
	7. The Star of David will be on the Israeli flag	Isa. 11:10
	8. The nation will be reestablished in the ancient land of Canaan	Jer. 30:2,3; Ezek. 37:12
	9. Israel will no longer speak of being freed from Egypt	Jer. 16:14,15
	10. Israel will not be restored as a monarchy	Mic. 5:5
	11. Israel will be established on the date predicted	Dan 4; Ezek. 4:4-6
	12. The Hebrew language will be revived in Israel	Jer. 31:23
	13. Jerusalem will be divided	Zech. 14:1-3
	14. Jordan will occupy the West Bank	Zeph. 2:8; Zech. 12:1-7
	15. Israel will be initially restored without Jerusalem	Zech. 12:1-7
	16. Israel will have a fierce military (firepot)	Zech. 12:1-7; Isa. 41
	17. Dead Sea Scrolls will be found	Isa. 29:1-4
	18. Israel will be reestablished by the fourth craftsman	Zech 1:18-21
	19. The Jewish people will come back in unbelief	Ezek. 37:7-8,11
	20. First shepherd will arise	Mic. 5:5-8
1949	21. Yemenite Jews will return	Isa. 43:3-7
1951	22. Israel will control Ashkelon	Zech. 9:1-8
1953	23. Egypt will no longer have kings (Suez crises)	Zech. 10:9-11

Recently Fulfilled Prophecies

1967	24. Second shepherd will arise	Mic. 5:5-8
	25. The 1967 war will occur on the date predicted	Dan. 5
	26. Five Egyptian cities will be conquered by the Israelis	Isa. 19:16-18
	27. Jordan will give up the West Bank	Zech. 12:6
	28. West Bank Jews will go home to Jerusalem	Zech. 12:6
1968	29. Israel will control Ashdod	Zech. 9:1-8
1973	30. Yom Kippur War will occur	Mic. 5:5-8
	31. Jerusalem will be a burden to all nations	Zech. 12:2,3
1980	32. The shekel will be revived as Israeli currency	Ezek. 45:1,2
1981	33. Third shepherd will arise	Mic. 5:5-8
	34. Israel will attack Iraqi (Nuclear) facility	Mic. 5:5-8
1982	35. Israel will give back the Sinai Peninsula	Zech. 10:6
	36. First Lebanese war will occur (firepot)	Zech. 12:6
1989	37. The Berlin Wall will fall	Ezek. 38:4-6
1990	38. Ethiopian Jews will be brought to Israel	Isa. 18:1-7
~2000	39. Cities will be restored, and Israel will have non-Jewish farmers	Isa. 61:4,5; Zeph. 2
	40. Jerusalem will grow beyond its old walls	Zech. 2:4,5
	41. Land of Israel will be divided by its rivers and by Muslims	Isa. 18:1-7
	42. Tourists will fly in and support Israel	Isa. 60:8-10; Isa. 61
	43. There will be constant planting and reaping (crops)	Amos 9:13-15
	44. Forests will reappear in Israel (cedar, etc)	Isa. 41:18-20
	45. Desolate land and cities will be restored	Ezek. 36:33-36
	46. Five cities will stay desolate	Matt. 11:20-24
	47. Muslims will not "reckon Israel among nations"	Num. 23:9
	48. Israel will inherit remnant of Edom /Palestinians	Amos 9:12
	49. Satellite-television communication systems invented	Rev. 17:8
2004	50. Sanhedrin will be reestablished	Matt. 24:15,20
2005	51. Palestinians will want Jerusalem as their capital	Ezek. 36:2,7,10-11
	52. Gaza will be forsaken	Zeph. 2:4
	53. Russia and Iran will sign a military defense pact	Ezek. 38:3-8
2006	54. Second Lebanese war will occur	Psalm 83:1-18

The Rapture

The fifteen prophecies scheduled to occur after 2008 are given below.

Date	Prophecy	References
2008+		
	55. An independent state will be created out of the West Bank	Dan. 11:45
	56. Fourth shepherd's Syrian war will occur	Mic. 5:1-8
	57. Fifth shepherd's Syrian war will occur	Mic. 5:1-8
	58. Lebanon-Jordan war will occur	Zech. 10-11; Obad. 1:19
	59. Sephardic Jews will return to Israel, & populate the Negev	Obad. 1:20
	60. Sixth Shepherd's Syrian war will occur	Mic. 5:1-8
	61. Damascus will be destroyed	Isa. 17:1
	62. Gog-Magog war will occur immediately after Israel wins another war	Ezek. 38
	63. Rise of the ten nations occurs after the Gog-Magog war	Dan. 8,11
	64. Increased understanding of prophecies will occur	Dan. 12:4
	65. Children will be rebellious, and society will be materialistic	Mark 13:12 1 Tim. 3:23
	66. Jesus' words will never be forgotten	Mat. 24:15
	67. Christians will be hated for Jesus' name's sake	Luke 21:17
	68. The apostasy of the church will fully form	
	69. The Rapture of the believing church will occur	
	70. The seven-year tribulation will begin	

Other Books by Ken Johnson, Th.D.

- **Ancient Post-Flood History,**
  Historical Documents That Point to a Biblical Creation.
- **Ancient Seder Olam,**
  A Christian Translation of the 2000-year-old Scroll
- **Ancient Prophecies Revealed,**
  500 Prophecies Listed in Order of When They Were Fulfilled
- **Ancient Book of Jasher,**
  Referenced in Joshua 10:13; 2 Samuel 1:18; 2 Timothy 3:8
- **Third Corinthians,**
  Ancient Gnostics and the End of the World
- **Ancient Paganism,**
  The Sorcery of the Fallen Angels
- **The Rapture,**
  The Pretribulational Rapture of the Church Viewed from the Bible and the Ancient Church
- **Ancient Epistle of Barnabas,**
  His Life and Teaching
- **The Ancient Church Fathers,**
  What the Disciples of the Apostles Taught
- **Ancient Book of Daniel**
- **Ancient Epistles of John and Jude**
- **Ancient Messianic Festivals,**
  And the Prophecies They Reveal
- **Ancient Word of God**
- **Cults and the Trinity**
- **Ancient Book of Enoch**
- **Ancient Epistles of Timothy and Titus**
- **Fallen Angels**
- **Ancient Book of Jubilees**

The Rapture
- **The Gnostic Origins of Calvinism**
- **The Gnostic Origins of Roman Catholicism**
- **Demonic Gospels**
- **The Pre-Flood Origins of Astrology**
- **The End-Times by the Church Fathers**
- **Ancient Book of Gad the Seer**
- **Ancient Apocalypse of Ezra,**
  called 2 Esdras in the KJV 1611
- **Ancient Testaments of the Patriarchs,**
  Autobiographies from the Dead Sea Scrolls
- **Ancient Law of Kings,**
  Noahide Law

For more information, visit us at:

Biblefacts.org

Bibliography

1. Cruse, C. F., *Eusebius' Ecclesiastical History*, Hendrickson Publishers, 1998.
2. Eerdmans publishing, *Ante-Nicene Fathers*, Eerdmans publishing, 1886.
3. Whiston, William, *The Works of Flavius Josephus*, London, Miller & Sowerby, 1987. Includes Antiquies of the Jews.
4. Ken Johnson, *Ancient Post-flood History*, Createspace, 2010
5. Ken Johnson, *Ancient Seder Olam*, Createspace, 2006
6. Ken Johnson, *Ancient Book of Jasher*, Createspace, 2008
7. Ken Johnson, *Ancient Prophecies Revealed*, Createspace, 2008
8. Ken Johnson, *Ancient Paganism*, Createspace, 2009
9. Ken Johnson, *Ancient Book of Enoch*, Createspace, 2012
10. Ken Johnson, *Ancient Book of Gad the Seer*, Createspace, 2016
11. Ken Johnson, *Ancient Apocalypse of Ezra*, Createspace, 2017

CPSIA information can be obtained
at www.ICGtesting.com
Printed in the USA
LVHW041110120719
623908LV00004B/46

9 781448 627639